SALADS

Better Homes and Gardens

TRADEMARK

TREASURE PRESS

BETTER HOMES AND GARDENS BOOKS

Editor Gerald M. Knox
Art Director Ernest Shelton
Managing Editor David A. Kirchner
Department Head, Cook Books Sharyl Heiken
Project Editors James D. Blume, Marsha Jahns
Project Managers Liz Anderson, Jennifer Speer Ramundt, Angela K. Renkoski

This edition first published in Great Britain in 1990 by:

Treasure Press
Michelin House
81 Fulham Road
London SW3 6RB

Original edition published by Meredith Corporation in the United States of America.

BETTER HOMES AND GARDENS is a registered trademark in Canada, New Zealand, South Africa, and other countries

ISBN 1 85051 506 9

Typeset by Servis Filmsetting

Printed in Hong Kong

Salads fit *every* occasion. Toss them or tote them. Make them elegant and sophisticated or quick and casual. Make them a main dish or simply make them ahead. Serve them before the dinner entrée, as a main course for lunch, or as a side dish with supper. Light and refreshing, salads make any mealtime memorable.

So, sample a bowl of fresh greens delicately wilted in a hot bacon dressing or try a simple three-bean salad with a delightful dill marinade. Or, create an extravagant, shimmering jelly salad. No matter what your menu, you'll find lots of time-tested salads, as well as delicious new creations.

You decide what sounds best. Then, let *Salads* provide you with the know-how and the show-how to make *your* kind of salad.

Contents

Simple Tossed Salads

A wooden bowl filled with a variety of crisp greens topped with a rich salad dressing—it's enough to make your mouth water. Fresh salads like these are simple and always sensational.

Survey our selection of refreshing salads. You'll discover recipes that satisfy your discriminating palate, yet don't tax your time and energy.

Tomato-Parmesan Toss

Tomato-Parmesan Toss

This salad says simple sophistication when you top it off with your favourite purchased salad dressing or one of the delicious homemade dressings in this book.

Salad greens*
18 cherry tomatoes, halved
1 ounce (30g) grated Parmesan cheese
3 rashers bacon, crisp-cooked, drained, and crumbled, *or* 3 tablespoons packaged bacon pieces
4 fluid ounces (115ml) desired salad dressing

Core Webb's Wonder lettuce; remove core (see photo 1). Rinse head under running water (see photo 2). Place, core end down, in colander to drain. If using other greens, rinse under running water. Remove stem from spinach. Remove centre vein from Cos leaves (see photo 3). Pat greens dry (see photo 4).

Tear enough greens into bite-size pieces to measure 2 pints plus 8 fluid ounces (1 litre, 370ml). Place any remaining greens in a polythene bag or crisper. Store in the refrigerator.

In a salad bowl place torn greens and cherry tomatoes. Sprinkle with Parmesan cheese and bacon. Pour dressing over salad. Toss to coat. Make 6 servings.

*Choose from Webb's Wonder lettuce, garden or round lettuce, Cos, leaf lettuce, spinach, watercress, endive, escarole, sorrel, or rocket (see pages 114–117).

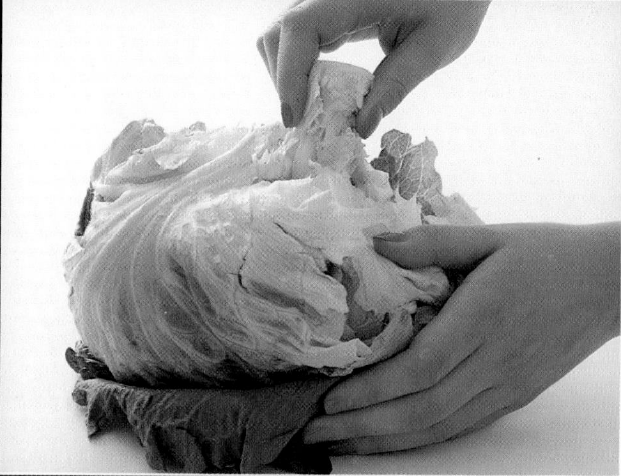

1 After purchase, check the lettuce for any wilted or discoloured outer leaves. Remove and discard them. Loosen the lettuce core by hitting the stem end of the head sharply on your kitchen countertop. Twist the core, then remove and discard it.

2 Place the head of lettuce, bottom side up, under cold running water. Rinse several times to clean the leaves. Drain the lettuce by inverting the head in a colander set in the sink or on a draining board. It will take about 15 minutes to thoroughly drain. Place the lettuce in a polythene bag; close securely and chill.

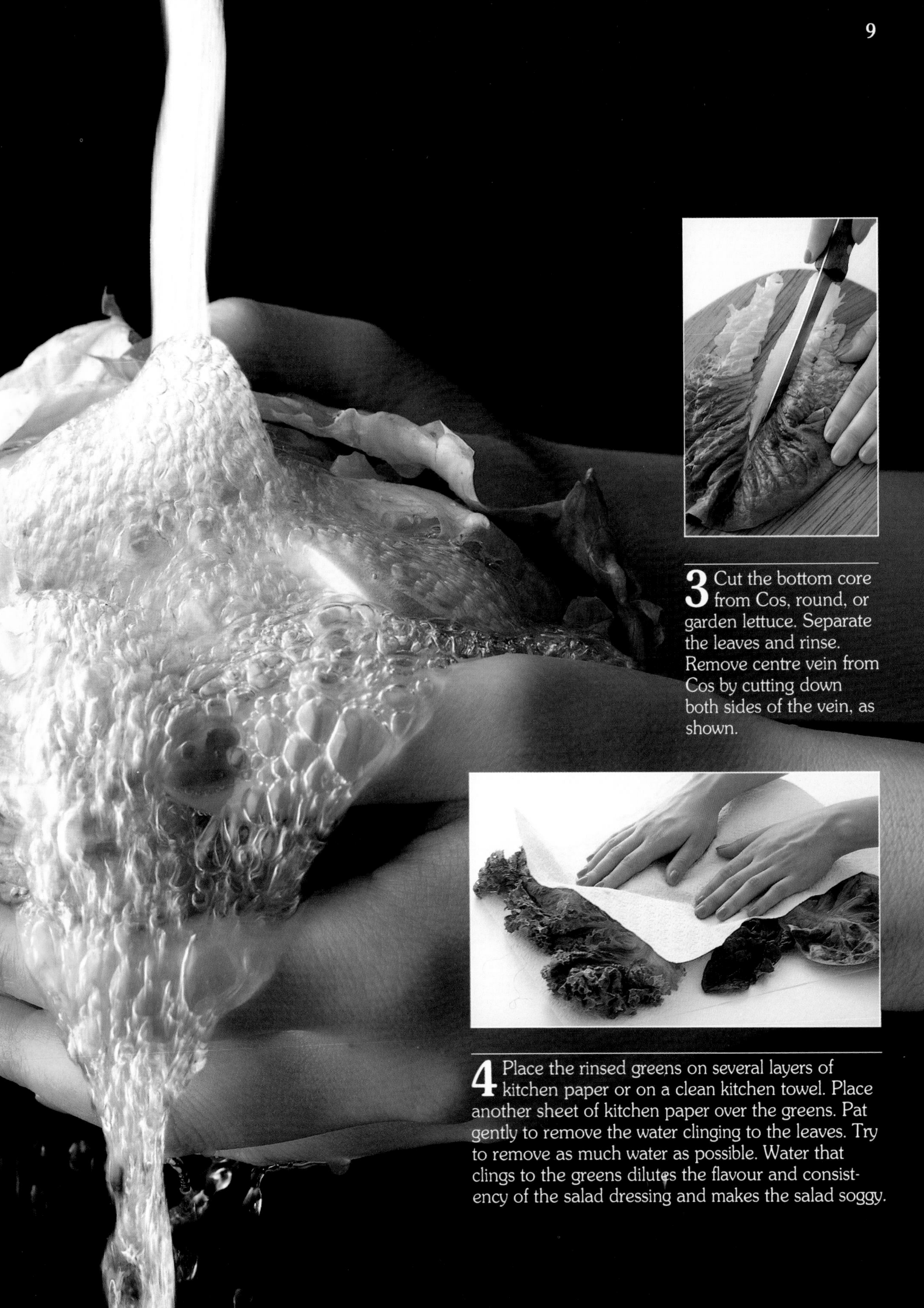

3 Cut the bottom core from Cos, round, or garden lettuce. Separate the leaves and rinse. Remove centre vein from Cos by cutting down both sides of the vein, as shown.

4 Place the rinsed greens on several layers of kitchen paper or on a clean kitchen towel. Place another sheet of kitchen paper over the greens. Pat gently to remove the water clinging to the leaves. Try to remove as much water as possible. Water that clings to the greens dilutes the flavour and consistency of the salad dressing and makes the salad soggy.

Chutney Salad

Chutney is a thick, sweet-tasting relish made from fruits or vegetables. Try apple or mango chutney for a fruity-tasting dressing.

8 ounces (225g) torn Cos *or* salad greens (see pages 8–9)
1½ ounces (40g) raisins
1½ ounces (40g) peanuts
2 fluid ounces (55ml) natural low-fat yogurt
2 tablespoons finely chopped chutney
1 tablespoon milk
¼ teaspoon curry powder

In a salad bowl place torn Cos or greens, raisins, and peanuts.

For dressing, in a small bowl stir together yogurt, chutney, milk, and curry powder. Pour dressing over salad. Toss to coat. Serves 4.

Crouton Salad Bowl

8 ounces (225g) torn round lettuce *or* salad greens (see pages 8–9)
2 ounces (55g) shredded Swiss cheese
1 ounce (30g) herb-seasoned croutons
2½ fluid ounces (55 ml) bottled Caesar salad dressing

In a salad bowl place torn lettuce or greens. Add cheese and croutons. Pour dressing over salad. Toss to coat. Makes 4 servings.

French-Onion Fling

To enjoy French-fried onions that are crunchy and crispy, serve this salad right after tossing it.

8 ounces (225 g) torn Webb's Wonder lettuce *or* salad greens (see pages 8–9)
2 ounces (55g) sliced fresh mushrooms
1 ounce (30g) tinned French-fried onions
2½ fluid ounces (70ml) desired salad dressing

In a salad bowl place torn lettuce or greens, mushrooms, and onions. Pour dressing over salad. Toss to coat. Makes 4 servings.

Beetroot-Spinach Salad

12 ounces (345g) torn spinach *or* salad greens (see pages 8–9)
8 fluid ounces (225ml) tinned sliced beetroot, drained
1 small onion, sliced and separated into rings
2½ fluid ounces (70ml) bottled Italian salad dressing
1 ounce (30g) crumbled blue cheese *or* shredded cheddar cheese

In a large salad bowl combine torn spinach or greens, beetroot, and onion. Pour dressing over salad. Toss to coat. Sprinkle with blue or cheddar cheese. Makes 6 servings.

Greek-Style Salad

The flavour of an olive oil ranges from sweet and mellow to sharp and distinct. The type of olive and its origin determine the flavour of the olive oil.

1 pound (450g) torn spinach *or* salad greens (see pages 8–9)
2 ounces (55g) crumbled feta cheese
8 ounces (225g) sliced pitted ripe olives
1 ounce (30g) broken walnuts
2 tablespoons lemon juice
2 tablespoons olive *or* salad oil
2 tablespoons honey
¼ teaspoon ground cinnamon

In a large salad bowl place torn spinach or greens, feta cheese, olives, and walnuts.

For dressing, in a screw-top jar combine lemon juice, oil, honey, and cinnamon. Cover and shake well. Pour dressing over salad. Toss to coat. Makes 8 servings.

Oriental Toss

Use the remaining water chestnuts for a stir fry. Just place leftover water chestnuts in a small container and cover with water. Cover and store in a refrigerator.

3 ounces (85g) frozen mange tout
8 ounces (225g) torn salad greens (see pages 8–9)
4 fluid ounces (115ml) tinned sliced water chestnuts, drained
1 tablespoon sesame seed
3 tablespoons salad oil
4 teaspoons vinegar
4 teaspoons dry sherry
2 teaspoons honey
2 teaspoons soy sauce

In a colander rinse mange tout under warm water to thaw. In a salad bowl place mange tout, torn greens, water chestnuts, and sesame seed.

For dressing, in a screw-top jar combine salad oil, vinegar, sherry, honey, and soy sauce. Cover and shake well. Pour dressing over salad. Toss to coat. Makes 6 servings.

Imaginative Webb's Wonder!

There's a wide variety of salad greens available in supermarkets today, yet Webb's Wonder lettuce remains a popular choice. In your next salad, go beyond torn lettuce and try some different shapes.

Wedges: Cut the head lengthwise in half. Place each half, cut side down, on a cutting board. Cut each half lengthwise into thirds. Makes 6 wedges.

Shredded: Cut the head lengthwise in half. Place each half, cut side down, on a cutting board. Cut crosswise into long, coarse shreds. Makes about 4 cups (680ml).

Rafts: Cut the head crosswise into 1-inch-thick (2.5cm) slices. Makes 4 to 6 rafts.

Chunks: Make rafts. Cut each raft crosswise and then lengthwise to get bite-size lettuce chunks. Makes about 4 cups (680ml).

Vegetable Salads

Crunch! Crispy, fresh vegetables make great-tasting salads. Follow along with us and we'll show you how to slice, dice, shred, and toss your way to home-style and company-special recipes.

Of course, the real fun comes when you sink your teeth into that delicious vegetable salad!

Vegetable Potpourri

Vegetable Potpourri

½ of a small head cabbage
¼ of a small head cauliflower
1 small courgette
1 stalk celery
1 small carrot
2 fluid ounces (55ml) soured cream
2 fluid ounces (55ml) bottled creamy cucumber salad dressing
1 teaspoon poppy seed
Dash bottled hot pepper sauce

Cut cabbage into quarters. Shred cabbage (see photo 1). Cut cauliflower into small flowerets. Slice flowerets, if desired (see photo 2). Cut courgette lengthwise in half, then cut into slices to form half-circles. Thinly bias-slice celery (see photo 3). Shred the carrot (see photo 4).

In a bowl combine cabbage, cauliflower, courgette, celery, and carrot. For dressing, in a small bowl stir together soured cream, bottled salad dressing, poppy seed, and hot pepper sauce. Pour dressing over vegetable mixture. Toss to coat. Makes 6 servings.

2 Rinse the cauliflower under cold running water. Using a paring knife, remove green leaves and any brown spots. Cut or break cauliflower into flowerets. If desired, cut flowerets into thin slices, as shown.

3 Hold the celery stalk firmly against a cutting board. Holding a knife at an angle to the celery stalk, thinly slice the celery.

1 For coarse shreds, hold a quarter-head of cabbage firmly against the cutting board. Using a knife, slice the cabbage to make long, coarse shreds, as shown.

For medium shreds, push a quarter-head of cabbage across the coarse blade of a vegetable shredder. For fine shreds use your blender, following the manufacturer's directions.

4 Use a coarse shredder to shred the carrot. Hold the carrot at an angle to the shredding surface. Rub carrot along the surface from top to bottom. Use this technique for other vegetables when you want long, pretty shreds.

Julienne Carrots: Cut a peeled carrot crosswise in half (You'll need to cut larger carrots into thirds.) Cut each carrot half or third lengthwise in half. Continue cutting each carrot stick lengthwise in half until they are thin, bite-size sticks.

You can also use this technique for cutting celery, cucumbers, courgettes, parsnips, turnips, meats, and cheeses.

Sweet 'n' Sour Salad

If you don't have a blender, quickly mix this dressing by hand. Just combine dressing ingredients in a small bowl and beat with a wire whisk.

1 large cucumber, cut into julienne strips (see tip box, page 15)
4 ounces (115g) coarsely shredded carrot (see photo 4, page 15)
1 tablespoon finely chopped spring onion
2 tablespoons vinegar
2 tablespoons orange juice
2 tablespoons honey
1 tablespoon salad oil
2 tablespoons sunflower seeds

In a bowl combine cucumber, carrot, and spring onion. For dressing, in a blender container combine vinegar, orange juice, honey, and salad oil. Cover and blend for 30 seconds. Pour dressing over vegetable mixture. Toss to coat. Before serving, sprinkle sunflower seeds over salad. Makes 4 servings.

Crunchy Coleslaw

Top this colourful coleslaw with rich Creamy Dressing or toss it with tangy Vinaigrette Dressing—either choice tastes superb.

10 ounces (285g) shredded cabbage (see photo 1, page 14)
2½ ounces (70g) broccoli *or* cauliflower flowerets (see photo 2, page 14)
2 ounces (55g) shredded carrot (see photo 4, page 15)
2 ounces (55g) chopped green pepper
2 tablespoons thinly sliced spring onion
Creamy Dressing *or* Vinaigrette Dressing

In a bowl combine cabbage, broccoli or cauliflower, carrot, green pepper, and onion. Pour Creamy or Vinaigrette Dressing over vegetable mixture. Toss to coat. Makes 6 servings.

Creamy Dressing: In a small bowl stir together 2 fluid ounces (55ml) *mayonnaise or salad dressing*, 2 teaspoon *sugar*, 2 teaspoons *vinegar*, ½ teaspoon *celery seed*, ¼ teaspoon *salt*, and ⅛ teaspoon *pepper*. Makes about 2½ fluid ounces (70ml) dressing.

Vinaigrette Dressing: In a screw-top jar combine 3 tablespoons *vinegar*, 2 tablespoons *salad oil*, 2 teaspoons *sugar*, ⅛ teaspoon *salt*, ⅛ teaspoon *garlic powder*, and 1 or 2 drops bottled *hot pepper sauce*. Cover and shake till combined. Makes about 2½ ounces (70ml) dressing.

Broccoli-Mushroom Salad

6 ounces (170g) broccoli flowerets (see photo 2, page 14)
$2\frac{1}{2}$ ounces (70g) sliced fresh mushrooms
2 ounces (55g) fresh bean sprouts
$2\frac{1}{2}$ fluid ounces (70ml) bottled Green Goddess salad dressing

In a bowl combine broccoli, mushrooms, and bean sprouts. Pour salad dressing over vegetable mixture. Toss to coat. Makes 4 servings.

Parsnip Salad

10 ounces (285g) shredded parsnips (see photo 4, page 15)
$2\frac{1}{2}$ ounces (70g) sliced radishes
$2\frac{1}{2}$ ounces (70g) finely chopped green pepper
2 ounces (55g) finely chopped celery
2 fluid ounces (55ml) natural low-fat yogurt
2 fluid ounces (55ml) bottled creamy Italian salad dressing
2 teaspoons sugar

In a bowl combine parsnips, radishes, green pepper, and celery. For dressing, in a small bowl stir together yogurt, bottled salad dressing, and sugar. Pour dressing over vegetable mixture. Toss to coat. Makes 4 servings.

The Chopping Block

It's puzzling to use a cookery book that has a recipe that calls for 5 cups of shredded cabbage, but says nothing about how much you should buy to get 5 cups. Refer to this handy chart when you're looking for yields of common vegetables.

Asparagus
1 pound (450g) = 2 cups (475ml) cut or snapped

Beans, green
1 pound (450g) = 4 cups (945ml) cut or snapped

Broccoli
1 pound (450g) = 6 cups (1 litre, 420ml) cut broccoli

Cabbage
1 pound (450g) = 1 small head, 5 cups (1 litre, 185ml) raw shredded

Carrots
1 pound (450g) = 6 to 8 medium carrots, 3 cups (710ml) shredded, $2\frac{1}{2}$ cups (590ml) diced, or $2\frac{1}{4}$ cups (530ml) chopped carrots

Cauliflower
1 small head = 4 cups (945ml) sliced or 3 cups (710ml) flowerets

Sweetcorn
1 ear = $\frac{1}{2}$ cup (115ml) cooked kernels

Mushrooms
1 pound (450g) = 6 cups (1 litre, 420ml) whole or sliced

Onions
1 large = 1 cup (225ml) chopped
1 medium = $\frac{1}{2}$ cup (115ml) chopped

Pepper, green
1 medium = 1 cup (225ml) strips or $\frac{1}{2}$ cup (115ml) chopped

Potatoes
1 pound (450g) = 3 medium or 2 cups (450ml) cubed, cooked

Spinach
1 pound (450g) = 12 cups (2 litres, 840ml) torn

Tomatoes
1 pound (450g) = 4 small
12 whole cherry = 1 cup (225ml), halved

Fresh Fruit Salads

It's easy to create a fruit salad packed with fresh-picked flavour. You'll see just how easy as you flip through this chapter. Here is an enchanting selection of salads bursting with assorted fruit: juicy apples, tangy oranges, and luscious peaches, to name a few.

In case you're short on time, we've given tinned fruit options for convenience. So, what are you waiting for? Start creating.

Ginger Fruit Bowl

Ginger Fruit Bowl

1 medium orange
1 medium apple*
1 medium peach*
2½ ounces (70g) strawberries
2 fluid ounces (55ml) pineapple yogurt
2 tablespoons mayonnaise *or* salad dressing
1 teaspoon brown sugar
¼ teaspoon ground ginger
Lettuce cups

Working over a small bowl, peel and section orange (see photo 1). Reserve orange juice. Place orange section in a mixing bowl.

Core apple (see photo 2). Coarsely chop apple; add to bowl. Peel peach (see photo 3). Thinly slice peach (see photo 4). Add peach to bowl. Remove hulls from strawberries (see photo 5). Halve berries; add to bowl. Toss fruit together.

For dressing, in the bowl with reserved orange juice stir together yogurt, mayonnaise or salad dressing, sugar, and ginger. Arrange lettuce cups on 4 individual salad plates. Evenly divide fruit mixture among the plates. Pour dressing over salads. Makes 4 servings.

*To keep cut fruits from turning brown, dip fruit in or brush fruit with a mixture of lemon juice and water or a mixture of water and ascorbic acid colour keeper.

1 Using a sharp paring knife, remove the peel and white membrane from the orange.
Working over a bowl to catch the juices, cut into the centre of the fruit between one orange section and the membrane. Turn knife down the other side of the section next to the membrane, as shown.

2 Wash the apple. Cut the apple lengthwise in half and then into quarters. Using a paring knife, cut down each side of the apple quarter along the core, as shown. Discard the apple core.

3 Insert a fork into the end of the peach. Dip the peach into boiling water for 20 seconds; remove.

While the peach is still on the fork, peel off the skin with a paring knife. Work from top to bottom, as shown. If the skin doesn't peel easily, return the peach to the boiling water for a few more seconds.

4 Cut the peach lengthwise in half. You don't have to remove the stone; just cut into slices, as shown.

In some peach varieties, plums, and apricots, you can insert the tip of a paring knife near the edge of the stone and gently lift the stone out.

5 Rinse strawberries. Remove strawberry hulls (also called caps) by inserting a paring knife under the hull of each strawberry, lift out the hull. Keep berries at their freshest by washing and hulling just before using them.

Date Waldorf Salad

The original Waldorf Salad was created by the maitre d' of New York's famous Waldorf Astoria Hotel. We've created our own version by adding dates and oranges.

2 medium apples, cored (see photo 2, page 20)
1 small orange, peeled and sectioned (see photo 1, page 20)
2 ounces (55g) stoned dates, snipped
1½ ounces (45g) sliced celery
1 ounce (30g) broken walnuts
4 fluid ounces (115ml) frozen whipped dessert topping, thawed
2 fluid ounces (55ml) mayonnaise *or* salad dressing
Lettuce leaves

Coarsely chop apples. In a medium bowl combine chopped apples, orange sections and reserved orange juice, snipped dates, sliced celery, and broken walnuts.

For dressing, in a small bowl combine thawed whipped dessert topping and mayonnaise or salad dressing. Spoon dressing over fruit mixture. Toss to coat. Line a serving bowl with lettuce leaves. Spoon salad into the bowl. Makes 6 servings.

Cranberry-Pear Salad

2 medium pears, cored (see photo 2, page 20)
1 medium orange, peeled and sectioned (see photo 1, page 20)
3 ounces (85g) seedless green grapes, halved
4 fluid ounces (115ml) tinned whole cranberry sauce

Coarsely chop pears. In a medium bowl combine chopped pears, orange sections, and halved grapes.

For dressing, in a small bowl stir together reserved orange juice and cranberry sauce. Pour dressing over fruit mixture. Toss to coat. Makes 4 servings.

Three-Fruit Salad

Choose your favourite honey for this delightful dressing. The source of the bees' flower pollen determines the taste, colour, and thickness of the honey.

2 medium peaches, peeled and sliced (see photos 3–4, page 21)
1 medium grapefruit, peeled and sectioned (see photo 1, page 20)
5 ounces (140g) strawberries, hulled (see photo 5, page 21)
2 fluid ounces (55ml) honey
1 tablespoon lemon juice
½ teaspoon poppy seed
Spinach leaves (optional)

In a bowl combine the sliced peaches, grapefuit sections, and strawberries.

For dressing, in a small bowl stir together honey, lemon juice, and poppy seed. Pour dressing over fruit mixture. Toss to coat. If desired, serve on a bed of spinach leaves. Makes 4 servings.

Easy Apricot Salad

Toast almonds by placing them in a 9-inch (23cm) pie plate. Bake in a 350°F (180°C) gas mark 4 oven for 10 to 12 minutes, stirring once during baking.

4 apricots, peeled and stoned (see photos 3–4, page 21), *or* 8¾ fluid ounces (250ml) tinned apricot halves, drained
1 small apple, cored (see photo 2, page 20)
Lemon juice
8 fluid ounces (225ml) tinned pineapple chunks, drained
1½ ounces (45g) thinly sliced celery
1 ounce (30g) flaked almonds, toasted
2½ fluid ounces (70ml) soured cream
1 tablespoon apricot preserves *or* orange marmalade
1 teaspoon lemon juice
¼ teaspoon ground nutmeg
2 cups torn lettuce *or* salad greens

Cut apricots into bite-size pieces. Coarsely chop apple. In a bowl combine apricots and apple. Sprinkle with lemon juice; toss to coat. Sitr in pineapple, celery, and almonds.

For dressing, in a small bowl combine soured cream, preserves or marmalade, 1 teaspoon lemon juice, and nutmeg.

Before serving, pour dressing over fruit mixture. Add lettuce or salad greens; toss to coat. Makes 4 to 6 servings.

Plum-Banana Salad

4 plums, stoned (see photo 4, page 21)
1 medium nectarine, peeled (see photo 3, page 21)
2 firm medium bananas
2 tablespoons lemon juice
2 fluid ounces (55ml) orange marmalade
2 teaspoons salad oil
¼ teaspoon poppy seed

Slice plums. Coarsely chop nectarine. Peel and bias-slice bananas. In a large bowl combine plums, nectarine, and bananas. Spinkle with lemon juice; toss to coat.

For dressing, in a small bowl stir together orange marmalade, salad oil, and poppy seed. Pour dressing over fruit mixture. Toss to coat. Makes 4 servings.

Cool Down

Try one of these cooling tips to make any of the salads in this chapter refreshingly cold.

•Chill ingredients thoroughly before you make the salad.

•Prepare the salad, cover, and chill for at least 1 hour.

•For a quick cool down, place the salad, covered, in your freezer for 20 minutes.

Super-Simple Main Dishes

With a flick of the wrists, these salads are ready. You can turn everyday egg salad into tantalizing Avocado and Egg Salad. Or, change humdrum ham salad into tropical Ham-Pineapple Salad.

Fix and feast in minutes or prepare your favourite salad ahead and chill till you're ready for a delectable dinner.

Broccoli-Salmon Salad

Broccoli-Salmon Salad

12 ounces (340g) tinned salmon
3 ounces (85g) small broccoli *or* cauliflower flowerets (see photo 2, page 14)
2½ ounces (70g) thinly sliced radishes
2½ ounces (70g) chopped celery
2 fluid ounces (55ml) mayonnaise *or* salad dressing
2 fluid ounces (55ml) soured cream
1 tablespoon sweet pickle relish
1 tablespoon milk
⅛ teaspoon pepper
Cos leaves

Drain salmon. Remove skin and bones; discard (see photo 1). Set salmon aside. In a large bowl combine broccoli or cauliflower, radishes, and celery (see photo 2).

For dressing, in a small bowl stir together manyonnaise or salad dressing, soured cream, pickle relish, milk, and pepper (see photo 3). Pour dressing over vegetable mixture. Toss to coat. Gently stir in salmon. Line 4 plates with Cos leaves (see photo 4). Spoon salad on to plates. Makes 4 main-dish servings.

1 Using your fingers, separate the tinned salmon into sections. Carefully remove the skin, bone, and cartilage; discard. Break the salmon into large chunks; set aside.

2 Add the sliced celery to the other vegetables. All the vegetables, but not the salmon, are added at this time. The salmon is added after the vegetables and dressing are combined. Adding the salmon last keeps it in large bite-size chunks.

3 Combine dressing ingredients in a separate bowl. Thoroughly mix the ingredients before adding dressing to the salad.

4 Arrange Cos leaves on one side of the dinner plate, as shown. If you're using an individual salad plate, arrange leaves in the centre and round the edges of the plate. The leaves add both colour and crunch to the salad.

Confetti Tuna Salad

8 ounces (225g) tinned tuna, drained and flaked
5 ounces (140g) shredded carrot (see photo 4, page 15)
5 ounces (140g) sliced celery
2 tablespoons finely chopped onion
3 fluid ounces (85ml) natural low-fat yogurt
2 teaspoons prepared mustard
¼ teaspoon pepper
1½ ounces (45g) chopped pecans *or* peanuts
Torn salad greens

In a large bowl combine tuna, carrot, celery, and onion (see photo 2, page 26). For dressing, in a small bowl stir together yogurt, mustard, and pepper (see photo 3, page 27). Pour dressing over tuna mixture. Toss to coat.

Before serving, fold in chopped pecans or peanuts. Arrange torn greens on 4 individual salad plates. Spoon salad on to greens. Makes 4 main-dish servings.

Ham-Pineapple Salad

8 fluid ounces (225ml) tinned crushed pineapple (juice pack)
11 ounces (310g) cubed fully cooked ham
3 ounces (85g) seedless red *or* green grapes, halved
1 ounce (30g) chopped green pepper
4 fluid ounces (115ml) natural low-fat yogurt
¼ teaspoon ground cinnamon
Dash ground nutmeg
Lettuce *or* spinach leaves

Drain pineapple, reserving *2 tablespoons* pineapple juice. In a large bowl combine drained pineapple, ham, grapes, and green pepper (see photo 2, page 26).

For dressing, in a small bowl stir together reserved pineapple juice, yogurt, cinnamon, and nutmeg (see photo 3, page 27). Pour dressing over ham mixture. Toss to coat. Line a serving bowl with lettuce or spinach leaves; spoon salad into bowl. Makes 4 main-dish servings.

Cheesy Prawn Salad

Personalize this recipe—substitute your favourite kind of cheese for the cheddar and Monterey Jack.

4 ounces (115g) cheddar cheese, cubed
4 ounces (115g) Monterey Jack cheese, cubed
5 ounces (140g) sliced celery
4½ fluid ounces (125g) tinned prawns, rinsed and drained
2½ ounces (70g) chopped green pepper
6 fluid ounces soured cream dip with toasted onion
1 tablespoon milk
¼ teaspoon dried basil, crushed
1½ ounces (45g) broken walnuts
Lettuce leaves

In a medium bowl combine cheddar cheese, Monterey Jack cheese, celery, prawns, and green pepper (see photo 2, page 26).

For dressing, in a small bowl stir together soured cream dip, milk, and basil (see photo 3, page 27). Pour dressing over cheese-prawn mixture. Toss to coat.

Before serving, stir in walnuts. Line a serving bowl with lettuce; spoon salad into bowl. Makes 4 main-dish servings.

Fruited Chicken Salad

If you don't have cooked chicken on hand, substitute frozen diced cooked chicken. Just thaw it and use as you would cooked chicken.

2 medium peaches, peeled and pitted (see photos 3–4, page 21), *or* 5 ounces (140g) frozen sliced peaches, thawed
11 ounces (310g) cubed cooked chicken
6 ounces (170g) stoned dark sweet cherries *or* seedless red grapes
2½ ounces (70g) sliced celery
4 fluid ounces (115ml) mayonnaise *or* salad dressing
½ teaspoon curry powder
⅛ teaspoon salt
2 firm large bananas
1 tablespoon water
1 tablespoon lemon juice
Leaf lettuce
2½ ounces (70g) cashews *or* peanuts
Coconut, toasted (optional)

Cut peaches into bite-size pieces. In a large bowl combine peaches, chicken, cherries or grapes, and celery (see photo 2, page 26).

For dressing, in a small bowl stir together mayonnaise or salad dressing, curry powder, and salt (see photo 3, page 27). Pour dressing over chicken mixture. Toss to coat.

Just before serving, slice bananas. In a small bowl combine water and lemon juice. Add bananas; toss gently to coat. Arrange lettuce on 4 individual salad plates (see photo 4, page 27). Arrange bananas on top of lettuce leaves.

Stir cashews or peanuts into chicken mixture. Place *one-fourth* of the chicken mixture on top of bananas on each plate. Sprinkle with toasted coconut, if desired. Makes 4 main-dish servings.

Avocado and Egg Salad

Have your hard-cooked eggs ever had a greenish ring around the yolk? You'll reduce the chance of getting these rings by carefully watching the cooking time. When the eggs are done, immediately place them in cold water.

6 hard-cooked eggs
1 large avocado, peeled and cut into cubes
1 tablespoon lemon juice
2½ ounces (70g) chopped celery
1 tablespoon sliced spring onion
2½ fluid ounces (70ml) mayonnaise *or* salad dressing
1½ teaspoons prepared mustard
¼ teaspoon salt
⅛ teaspoon pepper
Lettuce cups (optional)
2 rashers bacon, crisp-cooked, drained, and crumbled

Peel and coarsely chop eggs. In a large bowl combine avocado and lemon juice; toss. Add eggs, celery, and onion (see photo 2, page 26).

For dressing, in a small bowl combine mayonnaise or salad dressing, mustard, salt, and pepper (see photo 3, page 27). Pour dressing over egg mixture. Toss to coat.

To serve, spoon salad into individual lettuce cups, if desired. Sprinkle crumbled bacon on top. Makes 3 main-dish servings.

Frosty Fruit Salads

When you want something cold and refreshing, think of a frosty frozen salad. These super salads can work double-duty, too. Consider using them for a side-dish salad or as an enticing dessert.

Just mix up your favourite frozen salad and slide it into the freezer. The next time you're in the mood for something cool and creamy to soothe you, reach for a frosty salad.

Avocado Fruit Freeze

Avocado Fruit Freeze

Loaded with oodles of cream cheese and soured cream, this salad says "creamy"!

1 avocado, halved, seeded, and peeled
1 tablespoon lemon juice
8 fluid ounces (225ml) tinned jellied cranberry sauce
3 ounces (85g) cream cheese
2½ fluid ounces (70ml) soured cream
2 ounces (55g) sugar
8 fluid ounces (225ml) tinned crushed pineapple (juice pack), drained
Leaf lettuce

Chop avocado. In a bowl combine avocado and lemon juice; toss. Chop about *half* of the jellied cranberry sauce. Reserve remainder for garnish.

In a small mixer bowl combine cream cheese, soured cream, and sugar. Beat with an electric mixer till smooth. Fold in avocado, chopped cranberry sauce, and drained pineapple (see photo 1). Transfer mixture to a 9 × 5 × 3-inch (23 × 13 × 8cm) loaf pan (see photo 2). Cover and freeze 6 hours or till firm.

To serve, let salad stand at room temperature about 20 minutes to thaw slightly. Line 6 individual salad plates with leaf lettuce. Cut salad lengthwise in half, then crosswise to make 6 equal pieces (see photo 3). Remove with spatula to salad plates. Slice remaining cranberry sauce and cut into attractive shapes to garnish salads (see photo 4). Makes 6 servings.

Frosty Circles: Prepare Avocado Fruit Freeze as above. Spoon mixture into two 12 fluid ounce (345ml) or four 6 fluid ounce (170ml) juice concentrate cans. Cover and freeze. Let stand at room temperature about 20 minutes to thaw slightly. To remove salads, open bottom end of can and push salad out. Cut into 1-inch (2.5cm) thick slices. Serve as directed.

1 Gently fold the avocado, cranberry sauce, and pineapple into the beaten cream cheese mixture. Stir thoroughly to combine all the ingredients.

2 Transfer the mixture to a 9 × 5 × 3-inch (23 × 13 × 8cm) loaf pan. Using a rubber spatula or the back of a wooden spoon, spread the mixture evenly in the pan. Cover with foil or cling film.

Frosty Tropical Salad

Present this festive salad as either a side-dish salad or as a dessert.

8 ounces (225g) soft-style cream cheese with pineapple
4 fluid ounces (115ml) whipping cream
2 medium bananas, peeled and chopped
8 fluid ounces (225ml) tinned crushed pineapple (juice pack)
4 ounces (115g) glace cherries, finely chopped
1½ ounces (40g) chopped nuts
Lettuce leaves

In a small mixer bowl beat soft-style cream cheese with an electric mixer on medium speed for 30 seconds. Gradually add whipping cream, beating till fluffy.

Stir in chopped bananas, *undrained* pineapple, cherries, and nuts (see photo 1). Transfer fruit mixture to a 9 x 5 x 3-inch (23 x 13 x 8cm) loaf pan (see photo 2). Cover and freeze for 6 hours or till firm.

To serve, let salad stand at room temperature about 20 minutes to thaw slightly. Line 8 individual salad plates with lettuce leaves. Cut salad lengthwise in half, then crosswise to make 4 equal slices (see photo 3). Remove with a spatula to salad plates. Makes 8 servings.

3 Remove the salad from the freezer about 20 minutes before serving. This standing time allows the salad to thaw slightly so it's easier to cut. Using a sharp knife, cut the salad into squares.

4 Garnish each salad with the remaining cranberry sauce. Use small biscuit cutters or other small cutters to cut shapes from the cranberry sauce. Place the shapes on top of each salad.

Marinated Side-Dish Salads

You'll understand the saying "Great things come to those who wait" as soon as you sample these marinated side-dish salads. These salads let time work in your favour. Marinating them allows each salad to absorb the unique flavours of the marinade.

So, the next time you pack a picnic, take along Three-Bean Carrot Salad. Or, serve showy Marinated Mushrooms to those special dinner guests.

Three-Bean Carrot Salad

Three-Bean Carrot Salad

8 fluid ounces (225ml) tinned small whole carrots, drained
8 fluid ounces (225ml) tinned cut wax beans, drained
8 fluid ounces (225ml) tinned cut French beans, drained
8 fluid ounces (225ml) tinned red kidney beans, drained
1 small onion, sliced and separated into rings
1 small green pepper, seeded and sliced into rings
6 fluid ounces (170ml) vinegar
4 fluid ounces (115ml) salad oil
2 tablespoons sugar
½ teaspoon dried dillweed *or* 1 teaspoon dried savory, crushed
1 clove garlic, minced
Lettuce leaves (optional)

In a large bowl combine carrots, wax beans, French beans, kidney beans, onion rings, and green pepper rings.

For marinade, in a screw-top jar combine vinegar, salad oil, sugar, dillweed or savory, and minced garlic. Cover and shake well (see photo 1). Pour marinade over vegetables (see photo 2). Cover and chill 2 to 24 hours, stirring occasionally (see photo 3).

Line a bowl with lettuce leaves, if desired. Using a slotted spoon, remove vegetables from marinade to a bowl or a serving container (see photo 4). Makes 6 servings.

1 Combine the marinade ingredients in a screw-top jar. (A screw-top jar works best because you can shake it without spilling). Shake the jar well to thoroughly combine the ingredients.

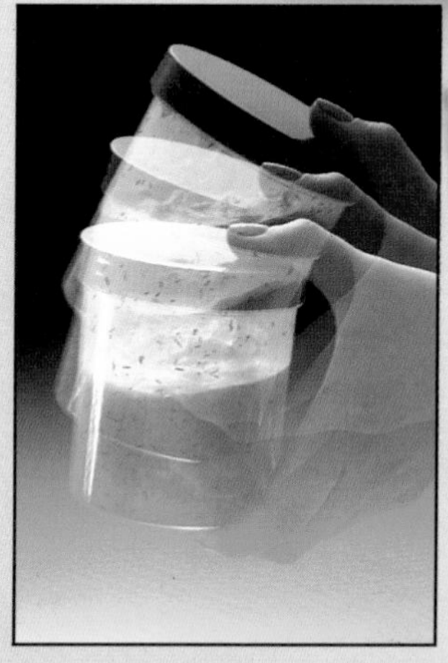

2 Pour the marinade over the vegetables. Use a spoon to stir the mixture and evenly coat all the vegetables.

3 Stir the vegetables occasionally during the marinating time. This helps to distribute the marinade and to coat all the ingredients.

4 To serve, use a large, slotted spoon to remove the vegetables from the marinade. The slots in the spoon allow the liquid to drain off the vegetables.

Marinated Mushroom

8 ounces (225g) fresh mushrooms, sliced
2 fluid ounces (55ml) white wine vinegar
1 small onion, thinly sliced
1 ounce (30g) chopped green pepper
2 tablespoons water
2 tablespoons salad oil
1 tablespoon French mustard
¼ teaspoon salt
¼ teaspoon dried basil, crushed
⅛ teaspoon pepper
7½ ounces (215g) coarsely shredded courgette, carrot, *or* lettuce

In a bowl toss mushrooms with vinegar. Add onion and green pepper.

For marinade, in a screw-top jar combine water, oil, mustard, salt, basil, and pepper. Cover and shake well (see photo 1, page 36). Pour marinade over vegetables (see photo 2, page 36). Cover and chill 2 to 24 hours, stirring occasionally (see photo 3, page 36).

Divide shredded courgette, carrot, or lettuce among 4 individual salad plates. Using a slotted spoon, remove vegetables from marinade to salad plates, reserving marinade (see photo 4, page 37). Drizzle about *1 tablespoon* of reserved marinade over each salad. Serves 4.

Caraway Cabbage Salad

1¼ pound (565g) shredded cabbage (see photo 1, page 14)
2 fluid ounces (55ml) bottle sliced pimiento, drained
1 ounce (30g) sliced spring onion
1 ounce (30g) chopped green pepper
2½ ounces (70ml) vinegar
2 ounces (55ml) salad oil
2 tablespoons water
1 teaspoon sugar
½ teaspoon caraway seed
¼ teaspoon salt
¼ teaspoon dried marjoram, crushed
⅛ teaspoon pepper
Parsley sprigs (optional)

In a large bowl combine cabbage, pimiento, spring onion, and green pepper.

For marinade, in a screw-top jar combine vinegar, salad oil, water, sugar, caraway seed, salt, marjoram, and pepper. Cover and shake well (see photo 1, page 36). Pour marinade over vegetables (see photo 2, page 36). Cover and chill 2 to 24 hours, stirring occasionally (see photo 3, page 36).

Using a slotted spoon, remove vegetables from marinade and place in a serving bowl (see photo 4, page 37). Garnish with parsley sprigs, if desired. Makes 6 servings.

Spiced Fruit Salad

Although allspice smells like a delicious combination of cinnamon, nutmeg, and cloves, the spice actually comes from the berry of an evergreen tree.

1 small pear, cored (see photo 2, page 20)
2 medium peaches, peeled, stoned, and sliced (see photos 3–4, page 21)
4 fluid ounces (115ml) orange juice
2 tablespoons honey
¼ teaspoon ground cinnamon
Dash ground allspice
Lettuce leaves (optional)
5 ounces (140g) strawberries, hulled and halved (see photo 5, page 21)
1 kiwi fruit, peeled and sliced, *or* 3 ounces (85g) seedless green grapes, halved

---

Cut pear into large pieces. In a large bowl combine pear pieces and sliced peaches.

For marinade, in a screw-top jar combine orange juice, honey, cinnamon, and allspice. Cover and shake well (see photo 1, page 36). Pour marinade over fruit (see photo 2, page 36). cover and chill 2 to 24 hours, stirring occasionally (see photo 3, page 36).

Before serving, line a serving bowl with lettuce leaves, if desired. Gently stir strawberries and kiwi fruit or grapes into marinated fruit. Using a slotted spoon, remove fruit from marinade to the lettuce-line bowl, reserving marinade (see photo 4, page 37). Pour 2 fluid ounces (55ml) of the reserved marinade over fruit. Makes 4 servings.

Dilled Vegetable Combo

4 ounces (115g) thinly sliced courgette
3 ounces (85g) sliced cauliflower flowerets (see photo 2, page 14)
2 small carrots, cut into julienne strips (see tip box, page 15)
2 tablespoons sliced spring onion
2 tablespoons snipped parsley
2 fluid ounces (55ml) white wine vinegar
2 fluid ounces (55ml) salad oil
1 teaspoon dried dillweed *or* ½ teaspoon dried savory, crushed
½ teaspoon celery seed
¼ teaspoon salt
⅛ teaspoon pepper
Leaf lettuce
6 ounces (170g) frozen mange tout, thawed
Snipped parsley (optional)

In a bowl combine courgette, cauliflower, carrots, onion, and 2 tablespoons snipped parsley.

For marinade, in a screw-top jar combine vinegar, salad oil, dillweed or savory, celery seed, salt, and pepper. Cover and shake well (see photo 1, page 36). Pour marinade over vegetables (see photo 2, page 36). Cover and chill 2 to 24 hours, stirring occasionally (see photo 3, page 36).

Line a platter with leaf lettuce. Before serving, stir thawed mange tout into vegetables. Using a slotted spoon, remove vegetables from marinade to the lettuce-lined platter (see photo 4, page 37). Sprinkle snipped parsley over salad, if desired. Makes 6 servings.

24-Hour Layered Salads

Fix and forget. These salads can be made and stored up to 24 hours before mealtime. Just prepare the salad ingredients and layer them. Then seal out the air and lock in the freshness with a creamy dressing. When you're ready to serve, the salad looks and tastes as fresh as if you just made it—greens and all.

Just toss it together or serve it in layers. From first forkful to last bite, all of these salads stack up!

All-American Layered Salad

All-American Layered Salad

Our version of this American picnic and potluck favourite has a delicate dill dressing capped by shredded cheddar cheese and tiny bits of ham.

8 ounces (225g) torn salad greens (see pages 8–9)
5 ounces (140g) shredded carrot (see photo 4, page 15)
1 ounce (30g) sliced spring onion
4 ounces (115g) frozen peas
8 fluid ounces (225ml) mayonnaise *or* salad dressing
2 tablespoons milk
½ teaspoon dried dillweed
3 ounces (85g) shredded cheddar cheese
1½ ounces (45g) finely chopped fully cooked ham

In the bottom of a medium bowl place torn greens (see photo 1). Layer in the following order: shredded carrot, spring onion, and frozen peas (see photo 2).

For dressing, in a small bowl combine mayonnaise or salad dressing, milk, and dillweed. Spread dressing evenly over top of salad (see photo 3). Sprinkle with cheese and ham. Cover tightly with cling film (see photo 4). Chill up to 24 hours. Makes 4 servings.

1 Arrange the greens in an even layer in the bottom of the bowl. The greens are put in the bottom of the bowl to keep excess moisture away from the vegetables and dressing.

2 Layer the remaining ingredients in the bowl: first the shredded carrot, then the spring onion, and finally the frozen peas. Try to keep the layers as even as possible. As the salad chills in the refrigerators, the peas will thaw.

3 Using a rubber spatula or knife, spread the dressing evenly over the pea layer, sealing the dressing to the edge of the bowl. The dressing layer helps seal out air, keeping the salad crisp and fresh.

4 Cover the salad tightly with cling film before chilling. This prevents the dressing from drying out and keeps the ham and cheese fresh. Ingredients that might become soggy or discoloured are sprinkled on just before serving.

Curried Fruit Salad

Using the purchased fruit bits is a real timesaver—they're already cut up.

8 fluid ounces (225ml) tinned crushed pineapple
12 ounces (345g) torn salad greens (see pages 8—9)
6 ounces (170g) mixed dried fruit bits
3½ ounces (100g) thinly sliced celery
11 fluid ounces (325ml) tinned mandarin orange sections, drained
4 fluid ounces (115ml) orange yogurt
¼ teaspoon curry powder
1 medium banana, sliced
1½ ounces (45g) coarsely chopped cashews

Drain pineapple, reserving *4 fluid ounces (115ml)* of the juice; set aside.

In the bottom of a large bowl or 3-quart (3-litre) casserole place *half* of the greens (see photo 1, page 42). Layer in the following order: dried fruit bits, celery, orange sections, remaining greens, and pineapple (see photo 2, page 42).

For dressing, in a small bowl combine reserved pineapple juice, orange yogurt, and curry powder. Spread dressing evenly over top of salad (see photo 3, page 43). Cover tightly with cling film (see photo 4, page 43). Chill up to 24 hours.

Before serving, arrange sliced banana on top of salad. Sprinkle with chopped cashews. Serve immediately. Makes 4 to 6 servings.

Layered Reuben Salad

Use rye melba toast to enjoy all the flavours of a hearty reuben sandwich.

8 ounces (225g) shredded cabbage (see photo 1, page 14)
4 ounces (115g) finely shredded lettuce (see pages 8–9)
8 fluid ounces (225ml) Thousand Island salad dressing
1 teaspoon caraway seed
6 ounces (170g) sliced corned beef, chopped
3 hard-cooked eggs, sliced
4 ounces (115g) shredded Swiss cheese
4 slices melba toast, coarsely crushed

In a mixing bowl combine cabbage, lettuce, *2 fluid ounces (55ml)* of the Thousand Island salad dressing, and caraway seed. In the bottom of a medium bowl or an 8 × 8 × 2-inch (20 × 20 × 5cm) dish place *half* of the cabbage mixture (see photo 1, page 42). Layer in the following order: *half* of the corned beef, remaining cabbage mixture, remaining corned beef, hard-cooked egg slices, and shredded cheese (see photo 2, page 42).

Spread remaining Thousand Island salad dressing evenly over top of salad (see photo 3, page 43). Cover tightly with cling film (see photo 4, page 43). Chill up to 24 hours. Before serving, top with crushed melba toast. Makes 4 main-dish servings.

Greek Layered Salad

We liked the colour contrast between the spinach and Webb's Wonder lettuce, but any salad greens you have on hand will work.

6 ounces (170g) torn spinach (see pages 8–9)
6 ounces (170g) torn lettuce (see pages 8–9)
3 ounces (85g) sliced stone ripe olives
2 ounces (55g) alfalfa sprouts
5 ounces (140g) cherry tomatoes, quartered, *or* 5 ounces (140g) chopped tomato
4 ounces (115g) crumbled Feta cheese
8 fluid ounces (225ml) natural low-fat yogurt
1 small cucumber, shredded
¼ teaspoon garlic salt
¼ teaspoon dried oregano, crushed

In a bowl combine spinach and lettuce. In the bottom of a medium salad bowl or a 12 × 7 × 2-inch (30 × 18 × 5cm) dish place *half* of the greens (see photo 1, page 42). Reserve *2 tablespoons* sliced olives; set aside. Layer in the following order: remaining olives, alfalfa sprouts, tomatoes, feta cheese, and remaining greens (see photo 2, page 42).

For dressing, in a small bowl combine yogurt, cucumber, garlic salt, and oregano. Spread dressing evenly on top of salad (see photo 3, page 43). Cover tightly with cling film (see photo 4, page 43). Chill up to 24 hours. Before serving, garnish with reserved sliced olives. Makes 8 servings.

Fiesta Salad

Tiny bits of fiery peppers in the Monterey Jack cheese add a spicy hotness to this salad.

6 ounces (170g) torn salad greens (see pages 8–9)
8 fluid ounces (225ml) tinned kidney beans, rinsed and well drained
4 ounces (115g) shredded Monterey Jack cheese with Jalapeño peppers
1 large tomato, seeded and chopped
2 ounces (55g) sliced stoned ripe olives
8 fluid ounces (225ml) soured cream dip with avocado
Several dashes bottled hot pepper sauce
3 ounces (85g) slightly crushed corn chips

In the bottom of a medium bowl or an 8 × 8 × 2-inch (20 × 20 × 5cm) dish place *4 ounces (115g)* of greens (see photo 1, page 42). Layer in the following order: beans, cheese, remaining greens, tomato, and olives (see photo 2, page 42).

For dressing, in a small bowl combine soured cream dip and bottled hot pepper sauce.

Spread dressing evenly over top of salad (see photo 3, page 43). Cover tightly with cling film (see photo 4, page 43). Chill up to 24 hours. Before serving, sprinkle with crushed corn chips. Makes 6 servings.

Grape and Pineapple Salad

4 ounces (115g) shredded *or* torn salad greens (see pages 8–9)
9 ounces (255g) seedless red *or* green grapes, halved
8 fluid ounces (225ml) tinned pineapple chunks (juice pack), well drained
2 fluid ounces (55ml) frozen whipped dessert topping, thawed
4 fluid ounces (115ml) natural low-fat yogurt
⅛ teaspoon ground cinnamon
1 ounce (30g) dessicated coconut, toasted

In the bottom of a small bowl or 1½-quart (1½ litre) casserole place greens (see photo 1, page 42). Layer grapes and pineapple (see photo 2, page 42).

For dressing, in a small bowl combine dessert topping, yogurt, and cinnamon. Spread dressing evenly over top of salad (see photo 3, page 43). Cover tightly with cling film (see photo 4, page 43). Chill up to 24 hours. Before serving, sprinkle with coconut. Serves 6.

Apple-Orange Salad

2 medium apples, cored (see photo 2, page 20)
2 tablespoons lemon juice
10 ounces (285g) torn salad greens
11 fluid ounces (310ml) tinned mandarin orange sections, drained
3 ounces (85g) cream cheese, softened
3 tablespoons orange *or* pineapple juice
Salted sunflower seeds

Cut apples into thin wedges, then toss with lemon juice. In the bottom of a 1½-quart (1½ litre) serving bowl place *half* of the torn greens (see photo 1, page 42). Layer in the following order: *half* of the mandarin orange sections, remaining greens, and apple slices (see photo 2, page 42).

For dressing, in a small mixer bowl beat softened cream cheese with an electric mixer till smooth. Add orange or pineapple juice gradually while beating. Spread dressing evenly over top of salad (see photo 3, page 43). Arrange remaining orange sections on top. Cover tightly with cling film (see photo 4, page 43). Chill up to 24 hours. Before serving, sprinkle with sunflower seeds. Makes 4 or 5 servings.

Chicken and Curry Salad

8 ounces (225g) shredded salad greens (see pages 8–9)
10 ounces (285g) cubed cooked chicken
2½ ounces (70g) raisins
1½ ounces (40g) sliced spring onion
2½ ounces (70g) thinly sliced celery
6 fluid ounces (170ml) mayonnaise *or* salad dressing
1 tablespoon chutney
½ teaspoon curry powder
¼ teaspoon paprika
Dash garlic salt
1½ ounces (40g) dry roasted peanuts, coarsely chopped

In the bottom of a medium bowl place *half* of the shredded greens (see photo 1, page 42). Layer in the following order: chicken, raisins, spring onions, celery, and remaining greens (see photo 2, page 42).

For dressing, in a small bowl combine mayonnaise or salad dressing, chutney, curry powder, paprika, and garlic salt. Spread dressing evenly over top of salad (see photo 3, page 43). Cover tightly with cling film (see photo 4), page 43). Chill up to 24 hours. Before serving, sprinkle with peanuts. Makes 4 main-dish servings.

◀ *Pictured opposite: Chicken and Curry Salad*

Savoury Vegetable Salads

Don't just dream of creamy potato salad, spicy bean salad, or any other vegetable salad favourite. Make yourself some! You'll love eating your vegetables when they're tucked in a tasty salad. They're truly irresistible!

Begin your salad with a savvy selection of vegetables, cooked to perfection. Then choose your dressing from a variety of tempting toppings. It's all designed to bring out the vegetable lover in you.

Italian Bean and Potato Salad

Italian Bean and Potato Salad

- 8 to 10 tiny new potatoes (1 pound, 450g)
- 9 ounces (225g) frozen Italian green beans
- 2 ounces (55g) sliced fresh mushrooms *or* 2½ fluid ounces (70ml) bottled sliced mushrooms, drained
- 2½ fluid ounces (70ml) bottled Italian salad dressing
- 1½ ounces (40g) sliced spring onion
- 3 rashers bacon, crisp-cooked, drained, and crumbled, *or* 2 ounces (55g) Parma ham, chopped
- 2 tablespoons grated Parmesan cheese

In a saucepan cook potatoes, covered, in boiling lightly salted water about 20 minutes or till tender (see photo 1). Drain; cool slightly. Cut potatoes in bite-size pieces (see photo 2).

Meanwhile, in a small saucepan cook green beans and fresh mushrooms according to package directions just till beans are crisp-tender (see photo 3). Drain.

In a large bowl combine potatoes, green beans, mushrooms, salad dressing, and spring onion. Cover and chill 2 to 24 hours. Before serving, sprinkle with bacon or Parma ham and Parmesan cheese (see photo 4). Serves 4.

1 Carefully insert a fork into one of the potatoes. If it's difficult to pierce the potato, the potato needs further cooking. When you can insert and remove the fork easily, the potato is tender.

2 Let the potatoes cool slightly. When they're cool enough to handle, place them on a cutting board. Cut each potato into small bite-size pieces. Leaving the peel on these tiny new potatoes adds vitamins and fibre, but whether to peel the potatoes is your decision.

3 Save yourself time and energy by cooking the green beans and fresh mushrooms together. Test the green beans by removing a bean from the saucepan; cool slightly. Bite into the bean. Beans should be tender, but still crisp. This stage is called *crisp-tender.*

4 Just before serving, sprinkle bacon pieces and Parmesan cheese over the salad. Adding these just prior to serving helps keep the bacon crisp and the cheese fresh.

Dilled Vegetable Vinaigrette

2 tablespoons water
2 tablespoons vinegar
2 tablespoons olive oil *or* salad oil
1 teaspoon sugar
1 teaspoon dried dillweed
¼ teaspoon dried savory, crushed
8 ounces (225g) sliced fresh mushrooms
2 medium carrots, cut into julienne strips (see tip box, page 15)
2½ ounces (70g) thinly sliced celery
2 medium tomatoes, sliced
4 leaves leaf lettuce *or* Cos

In a large saucepan combine water, vinegar, olive or salad oil, sugar, dillweed, and savory. Add mushrooms, carrots, and celery. Bring to boiling; reduce heat. Cover and simmer 5 minutes or till vegetables are crisp-tender (see photo 3, page 50). Pour vegetable mixture into a bowl. Cover and chill 2 to 24 hours.

Before serving, arrange tomato slices on 4 lettuce-lined salad plates. Using a slotted spoon, place *one-fourth* of the vegetable mixture on each plate, reserving vinaigrette mixture. Drizzle salad with vinaigrette mixture. Serves 4.

Creamy Potato Salad

6 medium potatoes (2 pounds, 900g)
5 ounces (140g) thinly sliced celery
2½ ounces (70g) finely chopped onion
4 ounces (115g) chopped sweet pickle
10 fluid ounces (285ml) mayonnaise *or* salad dressing
2 teaspoons sugar
2 teaspoons celery seed
2 teaspoons vinegar
2 teaspoons prepared mustard
2 hard-cooked eggs, coarsely chopped

In a saucepan cook potatoes, covered, in boiling lightly salted water about 25 minutes or till-tender (see photo 1, page 50). Drain; cool slightly. Using a paring knife, peel potatoes. Cut into bite-size pieces (see photo 2, page 50).

In a large bowl combine potatoes, celery, onion, and sweet pickle. For dressing, in a small bowl combine mayonnaise or salad dressing, sugar, celery seed, vinegar, prepared mustard, and 1½ teaspoons *salt*. Pour dressing over potato mixture. Toss to coat. Carefully fold in chopped eggs. Cover and chill 2 to 24 hours. Serves 8.

Sweet Potato and Pecan Salad

"Ya'll come and get it!" Here's a Southern-style salad made with sweet potatoes and toasted pecans, and tossed with a delicate orange dressing.

1 pound (450g) sweet potatoes
3 ounces (85g) cream cheese, softened
1 ounce (30g) snipped parsley
½ teaspoon salt
¼ teaspoon finely shredded orange peel
⅛ teaspoon pepper
2 fluid ounces (55ml) orange juice
2½ ounces (70g) thinly sliced celery
5 ounces (170g) chopped pecans, toasted

Cut large sweet potatoes into 2 or 3 pieces. In a saucepan cook sweet potatoes, covered, in boiling lightly salted water about 25 minutes or till tender (see photo 1, page 50). Drain; cool slightly. Using a paring knife, peel potatoes. Cut potatoes into bite-size pieces (see photo 2, page 50).

In a large bowl combine cream cheese, parsley, salt, orange peel, and pepper. Stir in orange juice, then mix well. Add potato pieces, celery, and pecans. Toss to coat. Cover and chill 2 to 24 hours. Stir gently before serving. Serves 4.

Perky Pototo Salad

3 medium potatoes (1 pound, 450g)
1 ounce (30g) snipped parsley
2 fluid ounces (55ml) olive oil *or* salad oil
3 tablespoons lemon juice
2 tablespoons thinly sliced spring onion
¼ teaspoon salt
⅛ teaspoon garlic powder
Several dashes bottled hot pepper sauce
Dash pepper

In a saucepan cook potatoes, covered, in boiling lightly salted water about 25 minutes or till tender (see photo 1, page 50). Drain; cool slightly. Using a paring knife, peel potatoes. Cut potatoes into bite-size pieces (see photo 2, page 50).

In a bowl combine parsley, olive or salad oil, lemon juice, spring onion, salt, garlic powder, hot pepper sauce, and pepper. Add potato pieces. Toss to coat. Cover and chill 2 to 24 hours. Makes 4 or 5 servings.

Tater Salad

3 medium potatoes (1 pound, 450g)
2½ fluid ounces (70ml) sweet pickle juice
2 teaspoons prepared mustard
2½ ounces (70g) chopped red *or* green pepper
2 hard-cooked eggs, chopped
1½ ounces (40g) thinly sliced sweet pickle
3 tablespoons chopped spring onion

In a saucepan cook potatoes, covered, in boiling lightly salted water about 25 minutes or till tender (see photo 1, page 50). Drain; cool slightly. Using a paring knife, peel potatoes. Cut into bite-size pieces (see photo 2, page 50).

In a large bowl combine pickle juice and prepared mustard. Add potato pieces, 2½ ounces (70g) red or green pepper, eggs, 1½ ounces (40g) sweet pickles, and spring onions. Toss to coat. Cover and chill 2 to 24 hours. Garnish with pickled pepper strips and pickled slices, if desired. Makes 5 servings.

Delectable Vegetables

Next time you're ready to start cooking vegetables, think micro-cooking. Both quick and easy, it's a great way to cook vegetables. Wash and trim vegetables (peel, if necessary). Place in a nonmetal dish or casserole; add 2 tablespoons *water*.

Cover with a lid or vented cling film. Micro-cook on 100% (HIGH) power for length of time indicated on chart. Stir or rearrange the vegetables once during cooking (stir courgettes twice). All timings are for 600- to 700-watt microwave ovens.

Broccoli spears (1 pound, 450g) 5 to 7 minutes

Broccoli cuts, ½-inch (1.25cm) pieces (1 pound, 450g) 6 to 8 minutes

Carrots, ¼-inch (.5cm) slices (1 pound, 450g) 7 to 9 minutes

Celery, chopped 5 ounces (140g) 5 to 7 minutes

Courgettes squash, ¼-inch (.5cm) slices (1 pound, 450g) 6 to 8 minutes

Mushrooms, sliced (½ pound, 225g) 2½ to 3½ minutes

Onions, ¼-inch (.5cm) slices (½ pound, 225g) 4 to 6 minutes

Peppers, green, chopped 2½ ounces (70g) 1½ to 3 minutes

Potatoes, quartered (1½ pounds, 680g) 12 to 15 minutes

Potatoes, new whole (¾ pound, 340g) 6 to 8 minutes

Refreshing Rice Salads

Once you've mastered the technique of cooking rice, you'll want to put your skills to use. Why not sample Fruity Rice Salad, featuring long grain rice and an enchanting curry flavour? Or, try Ham and Broad Bean Salad with chewy brown rice, bits of ham, and tender broad beans smothered in a creamy cucumber dressing.

Want more? Then turn the page for a look at recipes that help rice go beyond a hot side dish.

Oriental Rice Salad

Oriental Rice Salad

2½ ounces (70g) wild rice
14 fluid ounces (415ml) water
⅛ teaspoon salt
2½ ounces (70g) long grain rice
2 tablespoons salad oil
2 tablespoons rice wine vinegar *or* vinegar
2 teaspoons soy sauce
2 teaspoons honey
¼ teaspoon ground ginger
1½ ounces (40g) flaked almonds
6 ounces (170g) frozen mange tout

Rinse wild rice under cold water about 1 minute (see photo 1). In a small saucepan bring wild rice, water, and salt to boiling (see photo 2). Reduce heat. Cover and simmer 30 minutes. Stir in long grain rice (see photo 3). Return to boiling; reduce heat. Cover and simmer 15 to 20 minutes more or till water is absorbed and rice is done (see photo 4). Remove from heat. Let stand, covered, for 10 minutes.

For dressing, in a small screw-top jar combine salad oil, vinegar, soy sauce, honey, and ginger. Cover and shake well. transfer rice to a mixing bowl. Pour dressing over rice mixture. Toss to coat. Cover and chill 3 to 24 hours. Toast flaked almonds (see photo 5). Store in a covered container.

Before serving, place mange tout in a colander. Rinse mange tout under warm water to thaw. Add mange tout and toasted almonds to salad; toss to coat. Makes 6 servings.

1 Place wild rice in a strainer. (Make sure the strainer has small holes so the rice doesn't fall through.) Rinse the wild rice under cold water about 1 minute, lifting it with your fingers to rinse thoroughly. Rinsing the rice removes any dirt.

3 Stir in the long grain rice 30 minutes after the wild rice has started cooking. Long grain rice cooks faster than wild rice, so give wild rice a head start and they'll be done at the same time.

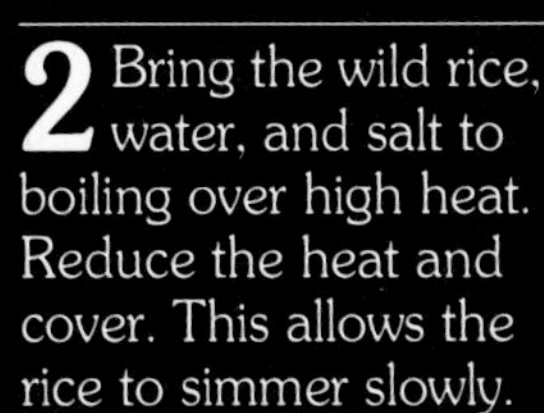

2 Bring the wild rice, water, and salt to boiling over high heat. Reduce the heat and cover. This allows the rice to simmer slowly.

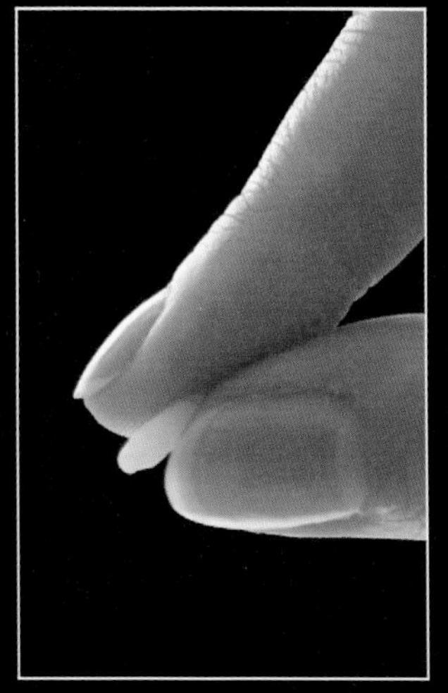

4 Test the long grain rice for doneness by pinching a grain (or a few grains) between your thumb and forefinger. If there is a hard core, cook the rice a little longer. Wild rice can't be tested this way, so cook it according to our timings.

5 To toast almonds, place them in a small skillet. Cook over medium heat, stirring constantly for even browning. The nuts will be golden brown in about 5 to 7 minutes. Remove them from the heat immediately.

Ham and Broad Bean Salad

You'll find the cooking time for brown rice is longer than that of long grain rice. Its chewy texture and nut-like flavour make it worth those extra minutes.

12 fluid ounces (355ml) water
4½ ounces (125g) brown rice
⅛ teaspoon salt
4 ounces (115g) frozen broad beans
8 ounces (225g) cubed fully cooked ham
1 small green pepper, coarsely chopped
1½ ounces (40g) thinly sliced spring onion
1½ ounces (40g) sliced stoned ripe olives
2 tablespoons snipped parsley
8 fluid ounces (225ml) bottled creamy cucumber salad dressing
Lettuce cups *or* lettuce leaves (optional)
2 hard-cooked eggs, sliced

In a small saucepan bring water, rice, and salt to boiling (see photo 2, page 67). Reduce heat. Cover and simmer 40 to 50 minutes or till water is absorbed and rice is done (see photo 4, page 67). Remove from heat. Let stand, covered, for 10 minutes. Cook broad beans according to package directions; drain.

In a bowl combine rice, broad beans, ham, green pepper, spring onion, olives, and parsley. Pour cucumber salad dressing over rice mixture. Toss to coat. Cover and chill 3 to 24 hours.

Before serving, spoon salad into lettuce cups or on to lettuce-lined plates, if desired. Top with egg slices. Makes 4 main-dish servings.

Mushroom-and-Bacon Rice Salad

2 ounces (55g) wild rice*
10 fluid ounces (285ml) water
⅛ teaspoon salt
2 ounces (55g) long grain rice*
3 ounces (85g) sliced fresh mushrooms
1 medium tomato, peeled, seeded, and coarsely chopped
3 rashers bacon, crisp-cooked, drained, and crumbled
2 tablespoons sliced spring onion
3 tablespoons salad oil
3 tablespoons lemon juice
1 teaspoon dried dillweed
¼ teaspoon garlic salt
Spinach *or* lettuce leaves

Rinse wild rice under cold water about 1 minute (see photo 1, page 66). In a small saucepan bring wild rice, water, and salt to boiling (see photo 2, page 67). Reduce heat. Cover and simmer 30 minutes. Stir in long grain rice (see photo 3, page 67). Return to boiling; reduce heat. Cover and simmer 15 to 20 minutes more or till water is absorbed and rice is done (see photo 4, page 67). Remove from heat. Let stand, covered, for 10 minutes.

In a medium mixing bowl combine rice, mushrooms, tomato, bacon, and spring onion.

For dressing, in a small screw-top jar combine salad oil, lemon juice, dillweed, and garlic salt. Cover and shake well. Pour dressing over rice mixture. Toss to coat. Cover and chill 3 to 24 hours. Serve on spinach- or lettuce-lined plates. If desired, garnish with additional tomato. Makes 6 servings.

***Note:** If desired, substitute 4 ounces (115g) *brown rice* for the 2 ounces (55g) wild rice and 2 ounces (55g) long grain rice. Cook brown rice 40 to 50 minutes, covered, or till water is absorbed and rice is done. Continue as directed.

Creamy Chicken-and-Rice Salad

8 fluid ounces (225ml) water
4 ounces (115g) long grain rice
1 teaspoon instant chicken bouillon granules
8 ounces (225g) cubed cooked chicken
2 medium tomatoes, peeled, seeded, and chopped
2½ ounces (70g) chopped celery *or* peeled, diced jicama
2 ounces (55g) frozen peas
8 fluid ounces (225ml) soured cream
3 tablespoons dry white wine
½ teaspoon salt
½ teaspoon dried tarragon, crushed
⅛ teaspoon pepper
4 lettuce cups
Parsley sprigs (optional)

In a small saucepan bring water, rice, and chicken bouillon granules to boiling (see photo 2, page 67). Reduce heat. Cover and simmer 15 to 20 minutes or till water is absorbed and rice is done (see photo 4, page 67). Remove from heat. Let stand, covered, for 10 minutes.

In a medium mixing bowl combine rice, chicken, tomatoes, celery or jicama, and peas.

For dressing, in a small mixing bowl combine soured cream, wine, salt, tarragon, and pepper. Pour dressing over rice mixture. Toss to coat. Cover and chill 3 to 24 hours. If necessary, add milk to moisten. Before serving, spoon salad into lettuce cups. Garnish with parsley, if desired. Makes 4 main-dish servings.

Fruit and Rice Salad

Go tropical! For another sensational flavour combination, substitute a tin of drained pineapple chunks for the mandarin orange sections.

10½ fluid ounces (310ml) water
4½ ounces (125g) long grain rice*
⅛ teaspoon salt
11 fluid ounces (310ml) tinned mandarin orange sections, drained
1 small apple, cored and chopped (see photo 2, page 20)
3 ounces (85g) seedless red *or* green grapes, halved
1½ ounces (40g) raisins
4 fluid ounces (115ml) natural yogurt
2 fluid ounces (55ml) mayonnaise *or* salad dressing
1 tablespoon chopped chutney
1 to 2 teaspoons curry powder
⅛ teaspoon salt
⅛ teaspoon pepper
3 ounces (85g) coarsely chopped peanuts
Cos or garden lettuce

In a saucepan bring water, rice, and ⅛ teaspoon salt to boiling (see photo 2, page 67). Reduce heat. Cover and simmer 15 to 20 minutes or till water is absorbed and rice is done (see photo 4, page 67). Remove from heat. Let stand, covered, for 10 minutes.

In a mixing bowl combine rice, mandarin oranges, apple, grapes, and raisins.

For dressing, in a small mixing bowl stir together yogurt, mayonnaise or salad dressing, chutney, curry, ⅛ teaspoon salt, and pepper. Pour dressing over rice mixture. Toss to coat. Cover and chill 3 to 24 hours.

If necessary, add milk to moisten. Before serving, stir in peanuts. Serve in lettuce-lined bowl or on lettuce-lined salad plates. Serves 8.

***Note:** If desired, substitute *brown rice* for the long grain rice. Prepare as directed, *except* use 12 fluid ounces (345ml) water. Cook brown rice 40 to 50 minutes, covered, or till water is absorbed and rice is tender. Continue as directed.

Jelly Gems

These yummy salads all start with packaged flavoured jelly. To this easy beginning add chunks of fresh fruit, bits of chopped nuts, or smooth, creamy yogurt.

The results: Salads in every colour of the rainbow. Sample some of these shimmering beauties, and find that each wiggle and jiggle explodes with flavour.

Strawberry and Apple Salad

Strawberry and Apple Salad

If you don't want to make shaky shapes from the jelly, pour the mixture into a 9 × 5 × 3-inch (23 × 13 × 8cm) jelly pan. Chill, then cut into squares.

10 fluid ounces (285ml) apple juice *or* cider
1 4-serving-size package strawberry-flavoured jelly
1 tablespoon lemon juice
8 ounces (225g) apple purée

In a saucepan heat *6 fluid ounces (170ml)* apple juice to boiling; remove from heat. Add strawberry-flavoured jelly; stir till dissolved (see photo 1). Stir in remaining apple juice and lemon juice (see photo 2). Chill till partially set (see photo 3).

Stir in apple purée (see photo 4). Line a 9 × 9 × 2-inch (23 × 23 × 5cm) pan or dish with cling film. Leave enough cling film to hang over the edge of the pan. Pour jelly mixture into the pan. Chill at least 6 hours or till firm. Before serving, cut jelly into shapes (see photo 5). Transfer to lettuce-lined salad plates; garnish with apple slices and decorate with mayonnaise and raisins, if desired. Serves 4 to 6.

1 Add the flavoured jelly to the hot liquid. Stir with a spoon to dissolve the jelly. Scrape the sides and bottom of the saucepan well to make sure all of the jelly granules are completely dissolved.

2 Stir the remaining apple juice into the jelly mixture. The second addition of liquid should be cold or at room temperature. This liquid cools the jelly mixture and starts the thickening process.

3 Place jelly in the refrigerator till partially set. At this stage, the consistency is similar to unbeaten egg whites. Or, chill jelly quickly by placing the saucepan in a large bowl of ice water; stir occasionally.

4 Stir the apple purée into the partially set jelly. Partially setting the jelly before adding the fruit helps keep the fruit distributed so it won't settle in the bottom or float to the top of the salad.

5 Carefully lift the cling film and jelly from the pan to a hard, flat surface. Use biscuit cutters to cut the jelly into shapes, placing the biscuit cutters as close together as possible. Cut through to the bottom of the jelly. Remove shapes with a spatula.

Lime and Grape Salad

8 fluid ounces (225ml) water
1 4-serving-size package lime-flavoured jelly
8 fluid ounces (225ml) white grape juice
1 medium banana, peeled and thinly sliced
3 ounces (85g) seedless red *or* green grapes, halved
Lettuce leaves (optional)

In a saucepan heat water to boiling; remove from heat. Add lime-flavoured jelly; stir till dissolved (see photo 1, page 72). Stir in white grape juice (see photo 2, page 72). Chill till partially set (see photo 3, page 73).

Stir in banana and grapes (see photo 4, page 73). Pour into a 9 × 5 × 3-inch (23 × 13 × 8cm) pan or six 6-fluid ounce (170ml) custard cups. Chill for at least 6 hours or till firm. If using a 9 × 5 × 3-inch (23 × 13 × 8cm) pan, loosen edges of salad with a knife, then cut into 6 pieces. Serve on lettuce-lined plates, if desired. Serves 6.

Very Berry Puff

Transform this salad into delightful dessert—just dollop each serving with frozen whipped dessert topping and sprinkle with toasted almonds.

8 fluid ounces (225ml) water
1 4-serving-size package raspberry- *or* strawberry-flavoured jelly
8 fluid ounces (225ml) raspberry *or* strawberry yogurt

In a saucepan heat water to boiling; remove from heat. Add raspberry- *or* strawberry-flavoured jelly; stir till dissolved (see photo 1, page 72).

Add yogurt. Transfer mixture to a small mixer bowl. Beat with an electric mixer on low speed till combined. Chill till partially set (see photo 3, page 73).

Beat with an electric mixer on high speed till doubled in volume. Pour mixture into an 8 × 8 × 2-inch (20 × 20 × 5cm) pan or six 6-fluid ounce (170ml) custard cups. Chill at least 6 hours or till firm. If using an 8 × 8 × 2-inch (20 × 20 × 5cm) pan, loosen edges of salad with a knife, then cut into 6 pieces. Makes 6 servings.

Cranberry-Orange Salad

A double dose of orange and cranberry gives the salad a tangy, festive flavour.

8 fluid ounces (225ml) cranberry juice cocktail
1 4-serving-size package orange-flavoured jelly
4 fluid ounces (115ml) cranberry juice cocktail
10 ounces (285g) frozen cranberry-orange relish, thawed
Lettuce leaves
Frozen whipped dessert topping, thawed
Orange slices (optional)

In a saucepan heat 8 fluid ounces (225ml) cranberry juice cocktail to boiling; remove from heat. Add orange-flavoured jelly; stir till dissolved (see photo 1, page 72). Stir in 4 fluid ounces (115ml) cranberry juice cocktail (see photo 2, page 72). Chill till partially set (see photo 3, page 73).

Fold in cranberry-orange relish (see photo 4, page 73). Pour into an 8 × 4 × 2-inch (20 × 10 × 5cm) pan. Chill at least 6 hours or till firm. Before serving, loosen the edges of the salad with a knife, then cut into 6 pieces. Place on lettuce-lined salad plates. Dollop with dessert topping. Garnish with orange slices, if desired. Makes 6 servings.

Golden Salad

Paper-thin pieces of bark from the cinnamon tree are used to make what we know as stick cinnamon. Stick cinnamon and whole cloves in this recipe give the salad a delicate spice flavour without clouding the jelly.

8 fluid ounces (225ml) unsweetened pineapple *or* orange juice
1½ ounces (40g) light raisins
2 3-inch (8cm) pieces stick cinnamon
4 whole cloves
1 4-serving-size package orange-pineapple-flavoured jelly
8 fluid ounces (225ml) ginger ale
11 fluid ounces (310ml) tinned pineapple chunks and mandarin orange sections, drained

In a small saucepan combine pineapple or orange jucie, raisins, stick cinnamon, and cloves. Bring to boiling; cover. Reduce heat; simmer for 5 minutes. Remove from heat. Remove spices.

Add orange-pineapple-flavoured jelly; stir till dissolved (see photo 1, page 72). Stir in ginger ale (see photo 2, page 72). Chill till partially set (see photo 3, page 73).

Stir in pineapple and orange sections (see photo 4, page 73). Pour into an 8 × 8 × 2-inch (20 × 20 × 5cm) pan or a 1-quart (1 litre) serving bowl. Chill at least 6 hours or till firm. If using an 8 × 8 × 2-inch (20 × 20 × 5cm) pan loosen the edges of the salad with a knife, then cut into squares. Makes 4 to 6 servings.

Snappy Tomato Cubes

10 fluid ounces (285ml) tinned hot-style vegetable juice cocktail
2 tablespoons lemon juice
½ teaspoon Worcestershire sauce
Few dashes bottled hot pepper sauce
Dash garlic powder
1 4-serving-size package lemon-flavoured jelly
2½ fluid ounces (70ml) cold water
4 garden lettuce or Cos leaves
2 fluid ounces (55ml) soured cream *or* natural low-fat yogurt
2 tablespoons milk
1 tablespoon chopped green pepper *or* spring onion

In a saucepan combine vegetable juice cocktail, lemon juice, Worcestershire sauce, hot pepper sauce, and garlic powder. Bring to boiling; remove from heat. Add lemon-flavoured jelly; stir till dissolved (see photo 1, page 72). Stir in cold water (see photo 2, page 72). Pour into a 9 × 5 × 3-inch (23 × 13 × 8cm) pan. Chill at least 6 hours or till firm.

Before serving, loosen edges of salad with a knife, then cut into ½-inch (1.25cm) cubes. Arrange cubes on lettuce-lined salad plates.

In a small mixing bowl combine soured cream and milk. (*Or*, if using yogurt, omit milk.) Drizzle over salads. Sprinkle with chopped green pepper or spring onion. Makes 4 servings.

Moulded Jelly Salads

Add flair to your next meal with one of these glittering jelly salads.

Cool and refreshing, these tasty salads complement any lunch or dinner. Each salad stands on its own—no salad dressings needed here to add flavour! Just unmould and you're ready to enjoy.

Layered Vegetable Aspic

Layered Vegetable Aspic

Salad oil
2 $14\frac{1}{2}$ ounce (415ml) tins chicken broth
2 envelopes unflavoured jelly
1 teaspoon finely shredded lemon peel
2 tablespoons sugar
2 tablespoons dry sherry
6 ounces (170g) finely shredded cabbage
$2\frac{1}{2}$ ounces (70g) shredded carrot
1 tablespoon finely chopped spring onion
$\frac{1}{2}$ teaspoon dried dillweed
1 whole spring onion
4 ounces (115g) frozen baby peas

Lightly oil a 2-quart (2 litre) soufflé dish. In a saucepan combine *1 tin* broth, jelly, and peel. Let stand 5 minutes (see photo 1). Cook and stir over medium heat till jelly is dissolved. Stir in remaining broth, sugar, and sherry. Pour 2 fluid ounces (55ml) jelly into soufflé dish. Chill till almost firm.

Meanwhile, in a bowl combine cabbage, carrot, chopped onion, and dillweed; set aside. Cook whole spring onion in boiling water 30 seconds or till limp. Place onion on jelly layer in soufflé dish, fanning out top of onion. Arrange peas over jelly layer (see photo 2). Pour *4 fluid ounces (115ml)* of jelly over peas; chill till almost firm.

Meanwhile, chill remaining jelly till partially set (see photo 3). Stir cabbage mixture into partially set jelly (see photo 4, page 73). Carefully spoon cabbage mixutre over pea layer (see photo 4). Chill at least 6 hours or till firm. Unmould salad on to a serving plate (see photo 5). If desired, garnish with lemon slices, mayonnaise or salad dressing, and parsley. Serves 6 to 8.

1 Sprinkle jelly over the chicken broth, as shown. Let stand for 5 minutes. This process is known as softening. During this time the jelly granules soften in the liquid so dissolving the jelly is easier.

2 Arrange peas evenly on the jelly layer. The jelly should be *almost* firm (sticky when touched). If the jelly is not almost firm, the peas will sink. If the jelly is too firm, the peas will not adhere to the jelly.

3 To quickly start the jelling process, place the saucepan in a bowl of ice and water. Using a spoon, stir the jelly mixture as it sets up.

4 Spoon the cabbage mixture over the almost firm pea layer. If the pea layer is not firm enough, the cabbage layer will mix with the pea layer. But, if the jelly has set too long, the two layers will not adhere to each other.

5 Dip the mould in warm water for a few seconds. Then, run a knife around the edge. Centre a plate upside-down over the mould. Holding the mould and plate together, invert them. Shake the mould gently and carefully lift it off. If the salad doesn't unmould, repeat the procedure.

Burgundy-Grape Mould

- Salad oil
- 8 fluid ounces (225ml) water
- 6 fluid ounces (170ml) frozen cranberry juice concentrate, thawed
- 2 fluid ounces (55ml) Burgundy wine
- 1 tablespoon honey
- 1 envelope unflavoured jelly
- 3 ounces (85g) cream cheese, cut up
- ¼ teaspoon finely shredded orange peel
- 1 orange, peeled, sectioned, and cut-up (see photo 1, page 20)
- 3 ounces (85g) seedless red *or* green grapes, halved
- Leaf lettuce (optional)

Lightly oil a 1½-pint (710ml) mould; set aside. In a saucepan combine water, cranberry juice concentrate, Burgundy wine, honey and jelly. Let stand 5 minutes to soften (see photo 1, pge 78). Cook and stir over medium heat till jelly is dissolved. Pour *6 fluid ounces (170ml)* of the jelly mixture into the mould. Chill till almost firm.

Meanwhile, pour the remaining jelly mixture into a blender or food processor container. Add cream cheese and orange peel. Cover; blend or process till smooth. Chill till partially set (see photo 3, page 73).

Stir orange pieces and grapes into partially set jelly (see photo 4, page 73). Carefully spoon over jelly layer in mould (see photo 4, page 79). Chill at least 6 hours or till firm.

Dip mould in warm water a few seconds to loosen edges. Unmould salad on to a serving plate (see photo 5, page 79). Garnish with leaf lettuce, if desired. Makes 4 to 6 servings.

Apple-Raisin Salad

These individual fruity salads are perfect any time you're looking for a light, refreshing salad.

- Salad oil
- 8 fluid ounces (225ml) apple juice
- 1½ ounces (40g) raisins *or* currants, chopped
- 1 4-serving-size package lemon- *or* orange-flavoured jelly
- 6 fluid ounces (170ml) cold water
- 1 small apple, cored and finely chopped (see photo 2, page 20)
- Leaf lettuce *or* spinach leaves (optional)

Lightly oil four *4 fluid-ounce (115ml)* moulds; set aside. In a saucepan combine apple juice and raisins or currants. Bring to boiling; remove from heat. Add lemon- or orange-flavoured jelly; stir till dissolved (see photo 1, page 72). Stir in cold water (see photo 2, page 72). Chill till partially set (see photo 3, page 73).

Stir apple into partially set jelly (see photo 4, page 73). Evenly divide jelly mixture among the moulds. Chill at least 3 hours or till firm.

Dip moulds in warm water for a few seconds to loosen edges. Unmould salads on to individual salad plates (see photo 5, page 79). Garnish with leaf lettuce or spinach leaves, if desired. Makes 4 servings.

Zippy Gazpacho Moulds

Presto, chango! We turned gazpacho, a cold soup made with tomatoes, green pepper, and cucumber, into a tantalizing salad.

Salad oil
2 fluid ounces (55ml) water
1 envelope unflavoured jelly
1 tablespoon lemon juice
¼ teaspoon onion powder
12 fluid ounces (345ml) tinned vegetable juice cocktail
2 ounces (55g) seeded and chopped cucumber
2 tablespoons chopped green pepper
Lettuce (optional)
Soured cream *or* mayonnaise (optional)

Lightly oil four 4 fluid ounce (115ml) moulds; set aside. In a saucepan combine water, jelly, lemon juice, and onion powder. Let stand 5 minutes to soften (see photo 1, page 78). Cook and stir over medium heat till jelly is dissolved. Add vegetable juice cocktail. Chill till partially set (see photo 3, page 73).

Stir cucumber and green pepper into partially set jelly (see photo 4, page 73). Evenly divide the jelly mixture among the moulds. Chill at least 3 hours or till firm.

Dip moulds in warm water for a few seconds to loosen edges. Unmould on to individual plates (see photo 5, page 79). Garnish with lettuce and dollop with soured cream or mayonnaise, if desired. Makes 4 servings.

Rum Fruit Moulds

Salad oil
3 ounces (85g) mixed dried fruit bits
4 fluid ounces (115ml) water
3 tablespoons light rum
1 4-serving-size package apricot- *or* orange-pineapple-flavoured jelly
8 fluid ounces (225ml) cold water
1½ ounces (40g) chopped pecans
Leaf lettuce (optional)

Lightly oil six 4 fluid ounce (115ml) moulds; set aside. In a saucepan combine fruit bits, 4 fluid ounces (115ml) water, and rum. Bring to boiling; reduce heat. Cover, then cook for 5 minutes; do not drain.

Add apricot- or orange-pineapple-flavoured jelly to fruit mixture; stir till dissolved (see photo 1, page 72). Stir in 8 fluid ounces (225ml) cold water (see photo 2, page 72). Chill till partially set (see photo 3, page 73).

Stir pecans into partially set jelly (see photo 4, page 73). Pour jelly into moulds. Chill at least 3 hours or till firm.

Dip moulds in warm water for a few seconds to loosen edges. Unmould on to individual salad plates (see photo 5, page 79). Garnish with leaf lettuce, if desired. Makes 6 servings.

Summertime Melon-Lime Mould

You can skip the softening step here. Just combine the sugar and jelly.

Salad oil
3½ ounces (100g) sugar
4 fluid ounces (115ml) water
1 envelope unflavoured jelly
1 envelope *unsweetened* lemon-lime-flavoured drink mix
10 fluid ounces (285ml) bottled ginger ale
9 ounces (255g) small honeydew melon balls
Vanilla yogurt (optional)

Lightly oil a 1½ pint (825ml) ring mould; set aside. In a medium saucepan combine sugar, water, jelly and drink mix. Cook and stir over medium heat till jelly is dissolved, then remove from heat. Slowly add ginger ale. Let stand 10 minutes, stirring occasionally. Skim off foam. Chill till partially set (see photo 3, page 73).

Stir melon balls into partially set jelly (see photo 4, page 73). Pour jelly mixture into the mould. Chill at least 6 hours or till firm.

Dip mould in warm water for a few seconds to loosen edges. Unmould salad on to a serving plate (see photo 5, page 79). Dollop with yogurt, if desired. Makes 4 to 6 servings.

Summertime Melon-Orange Mould: Prepare Summetime Melon-Lime Mould as above, *except* substitute 1 envelope *unsweetened orange-flavoured drink mix* and 9 ounces (255g) small *cantaloupe balls* for the lemon-lime flavoured drink mix and honeydew melon balls.

◀ ***Pictured opposite: Cranberry-Nog Mould***

Cranberry-Nog Mould

Salad oil
6 fluid ounces (170ml) cranberry juice cocktail
1 4-serving-size package raspberry-flavoured jelly
14 fluid ounces (400ml) bottled cranberry-orange sauce
2 fluid ounces (55ml) water
3½ teaspoons unflavoured jelly
1 tablespoon lemon juice
16 fluid ounces (450ml) dairy *or* tinned eggnog
6 fluid ounces (170ml) lemon *or* pineapple sorbets softened
Frosted cranberries* (optional)
Mint leaves (optional)

Light oil a 2-pint (1½ litres) ring mould; set aside. In a saucepan heat cranberry juice to boiling, then remove from heat. Add raspberry-flavoured jelly; stir till dissolved (see photo 1, page 72). Stir in cranberry-orange sauce. Pour cranberry mixture into mould. Chill till almost firm (see photo 3, page 73).

In a saucepan combine water, unflavoured jelly, and lemon juice. Let stand 5 minutes to soften (see photo 1, page 78). Cook and stir over medium heat till jelly is dissolved. Stir in eggnog and sorbet. Chill till partially set.

Carefully spoon eggnog layer over the cranberry mixture (see photo 4, page 79). Chill at least 6 hours or till firm.

Dip mould in warm water for a few seconds to loosen edges. Unmould salad on to a serving plate (see photo 5, page 79). If desired, garnish with frosted cranberries and mint leaves. Makes 8 to 10 servings.

***Note:** To frost cranberries, combine a slightly beaten *egg white* with a little *water*. Brush cranberries with egg white mixture. Sprinkle with sugar and place on rack to dry.

Wilted Salads

When you're hot you're hot—and these salads are definitely hot! A flash in the pan is all it takes to put together these wonderful wilted salads.

Crisp bacon and its flavourful drippings form the base for a subtly seasoned dressing. These last-minute salads are done in minutes. Just toss in the greens and in only moments your salad wilts to perfection.

Wilted Cos Salad

CANADIAN LAGER
BEER

Berry-Stuffed Papayas

To ripen papayas, let them stand at room temperature for 3 to 5 days or till the fruit yields to gentle pressure.

2 large ripe papayas
2 fluid ounces (55ml) lemon yogurt
1 tablespoon honey
2½ ounces (70g) strawberries, hulled and sliced (see photo 5, page 21)
2 ounces (55g) blueberries
1 large banana, sliced
1½ ounces (40g) nibbed pecans

Peel and halve papayas lengthwise (see photo 1). Scoop out seeds; scoop out pulp, leaving a ½-inch-thick (1.25cm) shell (see photo 2). Brush shells with *lemon juice*. Chop enough pulp to measure 4 fluid ounces (115ml) (see photo 3). Set aside. Reserve any remaining papaya pulp for another use.

In a mixing bowl stir together yogurt and honey. Stir in reserved 4 fluid ounces (115ml) papaya, strawberries, blueberries, and banana (see photo 4). Spoon filling into 4 papaya shells (see photo 5). Sprinkle with pecans. Serve on a lettuce-lined platter, if desired. Makes 4 servings.

1 Hold the papaya firmly in one hand. Using a paring knife, remove the peel from the papaya, turning the papaya as you peel. Then cut the papaya lengthwise in half.

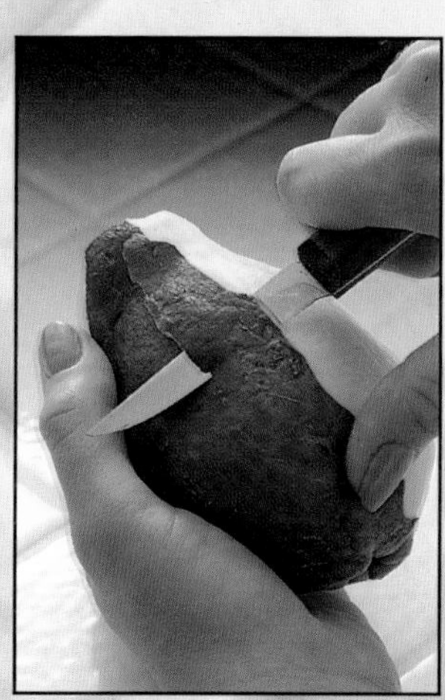

2 Using a spoon, scoop the seeds from the centre of the fruit; discard seeds. After the seeds are removed, continue to scoop out the pulp of the papaya with the spoon to form a ½-inch thick (1.25cm) shell.

3 Place the papaya pulp on a cutting board and chop into bite-size pieces. Use any remaining papaya soon as a dessert or snack.

4 Gently stir the fruit into the yogurt-honey mixture. Be careful not to break up the fruit as you stir, yet make sure all the fruit is coated with the dressing.

5 Spoon filling into each shell. Mound the filling on top and around the edges of the papaya as necessary.

Confetti Salad In Pepper Shells

In minutes you'll be ready to enjoy this creamy salad.

3 large green peppers
12 ounces (345g) cream-style cottage cheese, drained
2 fluid ounces (55ml) creamy cucumber salad dressing
4 ounces (115g) shredded carrot (see photo 4, page 15)
1½ ounces (40g) finely chopped celery
2 tablespoons sliced spring onion

Halve green peppers lengthwise. Remove stems. Scoop out seeds and membranes (see photo 2, page 90).

In a mixing bowl stir together cottage cheese and cucumber dressing. Stir in carrot, celery, and onion (see photo 4, page 91). Spoon filling into pepper shells. Chill, if desired. Makes 6 servings.

Chicken Salad In Tortilla Bowls

9 ounces (255g) frozen artichoke hearts
4 8-inch (20cm) flour tortillas
6 ounce (170g) torn salad greens (see pages 8–9)
10 ounces (285g) cubed cooked chicken
1 medium sweet red *or* green pepper, cut into 1-inch (2.5cm) squares
1 ounce (30g) sliced fresh mushrooms
2½ fluid ounces (70ml) mayonnaise *or* salad dressing
2 tablespoon dry white wine
⅛ teaspoon dry mustard

Cook artichoke hearts according to package directions; drain and chill. Meanwhile, brush 1 tortilla lightly with water to make it more pliable. Press tortilla into an ovenproof ½-pint (275ml) casserole. Repeat with remaining tortillas and 3 more casseroles. Place casseroles in a shallow baking pan. Bake in a 350°F (180°C) gas mark 4 oven for 15 to 18 minutes or just till crisp. Cool. Remove from casseroles.

Halve or quarter any large artichoke hearts. In a large mixing bowl combine artichoke hearts, torn greens, chicken, red or green pepper, and mushrooms; gently toss. Spoon filling into tortilla shells (see photo 5, page 91).

For dressing, in a small mixing bowl combine mayonnaise or salad dressing, Parmesan cheese, wine, and mustard. Pass dressing with salads. Makes 4 main-dish servings.

Fruit-Filled Nectarines

6 ounces (170g) watermelon balls *or* chunks
2½ ounces (70g) sliced strawberries, raspberries, *or* blackberries
1 ounce (30g) sliced celery
2 tablespoons honey
2 tablespoons lime juice
¼ teaspoon poppy seed
4 large nectarines *or* peaches
Lime juice
Lettuce leaves (optional)

In a medium mixing bowl combine watermelon, berris, and celery. For dressing, in a small bowl stir together honey, 2 tablespoons lime juice, and poppy seed. Pour dressing over fruit; toss to coat (see photo 4, page 91).

Halve nectarines or peaches; remove stone (see photo 4, page 21). If necessary, hollow out each nectarine or peach half, leaving a ½-inch-thick (1.25cm) shell (see photo 2, page 90). Brush shells with additional lime juice. Spoon filling into the 8 shells (see photo 5, page 91). Serve on lettuce-lined plates, if desired. Makes 4 servings.

Mushroom-Avocado Stuffed Tomatoes

4 large tomatoes
2½ fluid ounces (70ml) mayonnaise *or* salad dressing
1 to 1½ teaspoons prepared horseradish
⅛ teaspoon salt
Dash pepper
2 ounces (55g) sliced fresh mushrooms
2½ ounces (70g) chopped celery
1 medium avocado
Leaf lettuce (optional)
4 fluted mushrooms* (optional)

Cut a ½-inch (1.25cm) slice from the stem end of each tomato. Scoop out tomato pulp, leaving a ½-inch-thick (1.25cm) shell (see photo 2, page 90). reserve pulp. Discard seeds and juices; chop remaining tomato pulp (see photo 3, page 91).

In a mixing bowl combine mayonnaise or salad dressing, horseradish, salt, and pepper. Stir in tomato pulp, sliced mushrooms, and celery. Halve, stone, and peel avocado. Cut avocado into bite-size pieces. Stir avocado into filling mixture (see photo 4, page 91). Spoon filling into tomato cups (see photo 5, page 91).

If desired, arrange stuffed tomatoes on lettuce-lined salad plates. Garnish each with a fluted mushroom, if desired. Serve tomatoes immediately. Makes 4 servings.

***Note:** To make fluted mushrooms, hold a small sharp knife at an angle. Begin at the tip of the mushroom cap and carve a thin strip out of the cap in the form of an inverted "V". Turn the mushroom and continue cutting out inverted "V" strips in a spiral fashion, cutting out a total of 5 or 6 strips.

Salmon Salad in Bread Bowls

Save the bread you scoop out from the centre of the loaves to use in a favourite meat loaf or stuffing recipe.

1 16-ounce (450g) loaf frozen whole wheat bread dough, thawed
15½ fluid ounces (440ml) tinned salmon
2 fluid ounces (55ml) mayonnaise *or* salad dressing
1 tablespoon French mustard
¼ teaspoon dried dillweed
1 small cucumber, seeded and chopped
1 hard-cooked egg, peeled and chopped
2 tablespoons thinly sliced spring onion
3 ounces (85g) alfalfa sprouts
1 small tomato, seeded and chopped (optional)

Divide dough into 4 portions. Shape each portion into a small round loaf, 2¾ inches (7cm) in diameter. Place loaves on a greased baking sheet. Cover and let rise for 35 to 45 minutes. Bake in a 350°F (180°C) gas mark 4 oven for 20 to 25 minutes or till golden brown. Cool on a wire rack.

Meanwhile, drain salmon. Remove skin and bones; discard (see photo 1, page 26). Set salmon aside. In a mixing bowl stir together mayonnaise or salad dressing, mustard, and dillweed. Stir in cucumber, egg, and onion (see photo 4, page 91). Gently fold in salmon. Cover; chill.

Before serving, cut a slice off the top of each bread loaf. Hollow out bread loaves, leaving a ¼- to ½-inch-thick (.5 to 1.25cm) bowl (see photo 2, page 90). Line each bread bowl with one-quarter of the alfalfa sprouts. Spoon filling into bread bowls (see photo 5, page 91). Sprinkle with chopped tomato, if desired. Serve immediately. Makes 4 main-dish servings.

Dazzling Main-Dish Salads

What makes a main-dish salad really dazzle? In this case, it's the dressing. Start with creamy, homemade mayonnaise. From this modest beginning we show you how to make a variety of delectable dressings.

Underneath each dressing you'll find a hearty salad filled with fresh greens, crisp vegetables, and meats. Any one of these suppertime salads will fill you up and keep you going.

Seafood Salad

Creamy Mayonnaise

The flavour of this homemade mayonnaise in sandwiches and salads is well worth the effort.

1 large egg
1 tablespoon vinegar
½ teaspoon salt
¼ teaspoon dry mustard
⅛ teaspoon paprika
Dash ground red pepper
8 fluid ounces (225ml) salad oil
1 tablespoon lemon juice

In a blender container combine egg, vinegar, salt, dry mustard, paprika, and ground red pepper. Cover and blend about 5 seconds.

With blender running at low speed, gradually add 4 fluid ounces (115ml) salad oil (see photo 1). As necessary, stop blender and use a rubber spatula to scrape sides. Add lemon juice. With blender running at low speed, slowly add the remaining 4 fluid ounces (115ml) salad oil till mayonnaise is thick and smooth (see photo 2).

To store, transfer mayonnaise to a tightly covered jar. Store up to 4 weeks in the refrigerator. Makes about 10 fluid ounces (285ml).

***Note:** You can make Creamy Mayonnaise in your food processor. Prepare recipe as directed above, *except* double the ingredients.

1 With the blender running, gradually add the salad oil in a thin, steady stream, as shown. If the lid does not have a hole in the centre, lift the edge of the lid slightly and pour the oil slowly into the container. The oil must be added slowly to ensure a uniform, creamy emulsion.

2 The finished mayonnaise should be thick and smooth, as shown. If the mayonnaise does not form an emulsion, it will appear thin or curdled and will separate (see tip box, page 98).

Seafood Salad

If you're a real seafood lover, use half prawns and half crab meat in this salad.

2½ fluid ounces (70ml) Creamy Mayonnaise (see recipe, left)
2 tablespoons chilli sauce
2 tablespoons finely chopped spring onion
1 tablespoon snipped parsley
½ teaspoon lemon juice
Several dashes bottled hot pepper sauce
2 fluid ounces (55ml) whipping cream
10 ounces (285g) torn salad greens (see pages 8–9)
12 ounces (345g) frozen cooked prawns *or* crab meat, thawed
1 medium avocado
Lemon juice
2 medium tomatoes, cut into wedges
2 hard-cooked eggs, cut into wedges
Paprika (optional)

Prepare Creamy Mayonnaise (see photos 1–2, page 96). For dressing, in a mixing bowl combine 2½ fluid ounces (70ml) Creamy Mayonnaise, chilli sauce, spring onion, parsley, lemon juice, and hot peppr sauce. In a small mixer bowl beat whipping cream with an electric mixer on high speed till soft peaks form. Fold whipped cream into mayonnaise mixture (see photo 1). Cover and chill.

Evenly divide torn salad greens among 4 individual salad plates. Arrange prawns or crab on torn greens.

Halve, stone, peel, and sliced avocado. Brush avocado slices with lemon juice. Arrange avocado slices, tomato wedges, and hard-cooked egg wedges around seafood (see photo 2). Sprinkle with paprika, if desired. Pass dressing with salads. Makes 4 main-dish servings.

1 Gently fold the whipped cream into the mayonnaise mixture with a rubber spatula. This folding motion should be gentle, and should be done only till the two mixtures are combined.

2 Place prawns or crab meat on top of the torn salad greens on each individual salad plate. Space the seafood evenly around the plate. Then add the avocado slices, tomato wedges, and hard-cooked egg wedges.

More Salad Suppers

If you've been looking for a sensational main-dish salad, capped with a smooth, creamy dressing, look no further! Start with our basic Cooked Salad Dressing that you can jazz up. The result: a variety of delightful homemade dressings.

Need proof! Try one of the recipes in this chapter. We think you'll find the evidence simply delicious.

Scallop Salad with Pineapple Dressing

Cooked Salad Dressing

2 tablespoons sugar
2 teaspoons cornflour
1 teaspoon dry mustard
½ teaspoon salt
Dash ground red pepper
6 fluid ounces (170ml) milk
2 slightly beaten egg yolks
2 fluid ounces (55ml) vinegar
1½ teaspoons butter *or* margarine

In a small saucepan combine sugar, cornflour, mustard, salt, and red pepper. Stir in milk (see photo 1). Stir in egg yolks (see photo 2). Cook and stir over medium heat till bubbly, then cook and stir 2 minutes more (see photo 3). Add vinegar and butter or margarine; stir till butter is melted. Cool. Store in a tightly covered jar in refrigerator. Store up to 4 weeks in the refrigerator. If necessary, thin dressing with a small amount of milk. Makes 8 fluid ounces (225ml).

1 Add the milk all at once to the dry ingedients. Stir with a wooden spoon to thoroughly combine the milk and dry ingredients. Make sure the mixture is well-combined to avoid lumps.

2 Stir slightly beaten egg yolks into the milk mixture. The egg yolks help thicken the dressing and give it a rich, lemon-yellow colour.

3 Cook and stir the dressing over medium heat till bubbly, then cook 2 minutes more. This cooks the egg yolks and cornflour for maximum thickening power. The salad dressing will have a thick, creamy consistency and appear glossy.

Scallop Salad with Pineapple Dressing

4 fluid ounces (115ml) Cooked Salad Dressing (see recipe, left)
2 tablespoons orange marmalade
12 ounces (345g) fresh *or* frozen bay scallops
12 ounces (345g) frozen mange tout, thawed
1 pint plus 2 fluid ounces (650ml) tinned pineapple chunks and mandarin orange sections, chilled and drained
5 ounces (140g) bias-sliced celery (optional)
Pomegranate seeds (optional)

Prepare Cooked salad Dressing (see photos 1–3, page 102). In a small bowl combine 4 fluid ounces (115ml) Cooked Salad Dressing and orange marmalade. Cover and chill in the refrigerator.

Thaw scallops, if frozen. Add scallops to saucepan of boiling salted water. Simmer about 1 minute or till scallops are opaque and tender (see photo 1). Drain. Cover and chill.

Meanwhile, arrange mange tout on a serving platter or on 4 individual salad plates. Arrange scallops, pineapple and orange sections, and celery, if desired, beside mange tout (see photo 2). If necessary, thin dressing with a small amount of milk. Drizzle salad with dressing before serving. Garnish with pomegranate seeds, if desired. Makes 4 main-dish servings.

1 Add scallops to the boiling water. cook about 1 minute. The scallops are done when they change from transparent to opaque.

2 Arrange scallops on top of the mange tout. Top with the pineapple tidbits and orange sections and then the celery, if desired.

Salad Luncheon

When it's your turn to host the volunteer group or have the bridge club over, you'll be ready. Light and lush, this spread of salads will have your guests wanting to taste every dish—again and again!

Menu

- Caesar Salad*
- Ham Slaw Salad*
- Seafood Tabbouleh*
- Fresh Fruit Platter*
- Herb Twists*
- Lemon Bread*
- Minty Pineappleade*
- Iced Tea

* *see pages 108—113*

Caesar Salad

Caesar Salad

1 egg
1 clove garlic, halved
2 tablespoons olive oil *or* salad oil
2 tablespoons lemon *or* lime juice
Few dashes Worcestershire sauce
Dash bottled hot pepper sauce
10 ounces (285g) torn Cos lettuce
1 ounce (30g) Garlic Croutons
1 ounce (30g) grated Parmesan cheese
Dash pepper
Rolled anchovy fillets (optional)

Allow egg to come to room temperature. To coddle egg place whole egg in a small saucepan of boiling water (see photo 1). Remove from heat; let stand 1 minute. Drain and cool slightly.

Rub a large wooden salad bowl with the cut sides of garlic clove (see photo 2). Discard garlic. Add oil, lemon or lime juice, Worcestershire sauce, and bottled hot pepper sauce. Break the coddled egg into the bowl (see photo 3). Using a fork or a wire whisk, beat till the dressing becomes creamy. Add lettuce. Toss to coat (see photo 4). Sprinkle with Garlic Croutons, Parmesan cheese, and pepper; toss. If desired, top with anchovy fillets. Makes 6 servings.

Garlic Croutons: Spread both sides of four ½-inch-thick (1.25cm) *French bread* slices with 3 tablespoons softened *butter* or *margarine*. Sprinkle with *garlic powder*. Cut bread into ¾-inch (2cm) cubes (see tip box). Spread cubes on a baking sheet. Bake in a 300°F (150°C) gas mark 2 oven for 12 to 15 minutes or till croutons are dry-crisp. Cover and refrigerate. Makes about 1 pint (450ml).

1 Carefully lower the egg into boiling water. Remove the pan from the heat and let stand 1 minute. During this time the egg cooks slightly, coddling it. Drain and cool the egg.

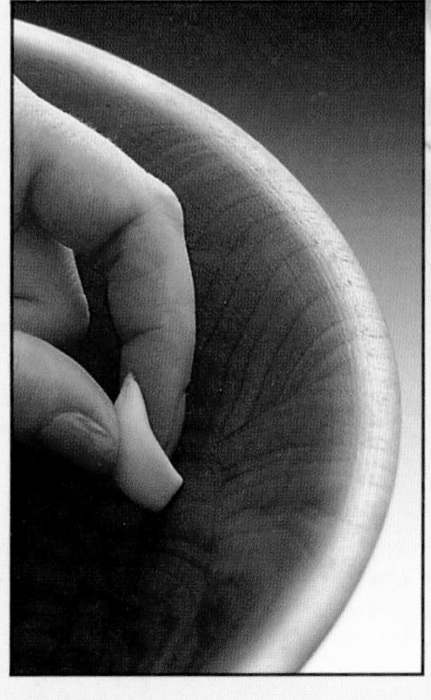

2 Using the cut sides of the garlic clove, rub the bottom and sides of the wooden salad bowl. This gives the salad just a hint of garlic without being too strong.

3 Break the coddled egg into the wooden bowl. With a fork or wire whisk beat the egg, oil, lemon or lime juice, Worcestershire sauce, and hot pepper sauce till creamy.

4 Add torn lettuce to the salad bowl. Using 2 salad servers or a salad fork and spoon toss the salad with a lifting motion. Toss till lettuce is thoroughly coated with dressing.

Croutons: Place the French bread slices on a cutting board. Using a sharp knife, cut each slice of bread into ¾-inch (2cm) strips then cut the strips crosswise into ¾-inch (2cm) cubes.

Timetable

1 day before

- Mix the base for the Minty Pineappleade. Pour mixture into a jar. Cover and chill.
- Prepare Lemon Bread; bake. Remove bread from pan and cool on rack. Wrap and store at room temperature, so it's fresh for the luncheon.
- Prepare Seafood Tabbouleh. Cover. Place in refrigerator to chill and let flavours develop.
- Make croutons for the Caesar Salad.

2½ hrs. before

- Prepare Ham Slaw Salad. Cover and chill.
- While the salad is chilling, set out plates, flatware, napkins, glasses, and decorations. Plan a simple, buffet-style table setting. Place everything in a natural progression: plates first, food next, and the flatware and glasses last. Help guests by setting out flatware wrapped in napkins.

50 mins. before

- Tear Cos lettuce for Caesar Salad.
- Prepare assorted fruits for Fresh Fruit Platter; brush with lemon juice, if desired. Make the dressing.
- Prepare Herb Twists and top with desired coatings. Bake. Meanwhile, coddle egg for the Caesar Salad.

15 mins. before

- Turn salads into serving bowls and garnish.
- Cut Lemon Bread into slices.
- Make dressing for the Caesar Salad and toss salad ingredients.

At Serving Time

- Place ice cubes in glasses. Add carbonated water to the Minty Pineappleade base; stir.
- Now, relax and enjoy your guests.

Ham Slaw Salad

12 ounces (345g) coarsely shredded green cabbage (see photo 1, page 14)
12 ounces (345g) diced fully cooked ham *or* corned beef
3 ounces (85g) chopped green pepper
2½ ounces (70g) shredded carrot (see photo 4, page 15)
2½ fluid ounces (70ml) soured cream
2½ fluid ounces (70ml) bottled creamy cucumber salad dressing
Cabbage leaves (optional)

In a bowl combine shredded cabbage, ham or corned beef, green pepper, and carrot. For dressing, combine soured cream and cucumber dressing. Pour dressing over cabbage mixture; toss to coat. Cover; chill 2 to 24 hours.

Before serving, spoon salad into a cabbage-lined bowl or hollowed-out cabbage, if desired. Makes 6 main-dish servings.

Herb Twists

No eggs on hand? Brush the roll ropes with milk, and then sprinkle on cheese, poppy seed, or sesame seed. (Pictured on page 106.)

20 refrigerated rolls
1 beaten egg
1 tablespoon water
Grated Parmesan cheese, poppy seed, *or* sesame seed, toasted

With hands, shape each roll into an 8-inch (20cm) rope. Moisten hands, if necessary (ropes will shrink to 6 inches (15cm). Twist 2 ropes together.

In a small bowl stir together egg and water. Brush tops of twists with egg-water mixture. Sprinkle with cheese, poppy seed, or sesame seed. Place twists on a greased baking sheet. Bake in a 375°F (190°C) gas mark 5 oven for 15 to 18 minutes or till golden brown. Makes 10 twists.

Fresh Fruit Platter

If you're looking to cut calories, enjoy this fruit platter with little or no dressing.

3 tablespoons sugar
2 tablespoons orange juice *or* unsweetened pineapple juice
½ teaspoon dry mustard
¼ teaspoon poppy seed (optional)
4 fluid ounces (115ml) salad oil
1 pint plus 4 fluid ounces (570ml) assorted fruit*

In a small mixer bowl combine sugar, orange juice or pineapple juice, dry mustard, and poppy seed, if desired. Add salad oil, a small amount at a time, beating with a rotary beater after each addition.

Arrange fruit on a serving platter in a decorative fashion. Pass the dressing; drizzle over fruit. Makes 6 servings.

*Choose from the following fruit: halved strawberries; blueberries; raspberries; sliced kiwi fruit; melon slices, balls, *or* cubes; peach *or* nectarine slices; pineapple chunks; orange sections; *or* sliced papaya *or* mango.

Lemon Bread

1 pound plus 1 ounce (480g) plain flour
4 teaspoons baking powder
2 teaspoons finely shredded lemon peel
½ teaspoon salt
1 beaten egg
6 fluid ounces (170ml) milk
5 ounces (140g) sugar
2 fluid ounces (55ml) cooking oil
1 tablespoon lemon juice

Grease an 8 × 4 × 2-inch (20 × 10 × 5cm) loaf pan; set aside. In a medium mixing bowl stir together flour, baking powder, lemon peel, and salt.

Combine egg, milk, sugar, oil, and lemon juice. Add to flour mixture, stirring just till moistened. Turn batter into prepared pan. Bake in a 350°F (180°C) gas mark 4 oven for 50 to 55 minutes. Cool in pan 10 minutes. remove from pan. Cool on wire rack. Wrap in foil or cling film; store overnight. Makes 1 loaf.

Minty Pineappleade

2 small pineapples *or* 1 pint (450ml) tinned crushed pineapple (juice pack)*
7 ounces (200g) sugar
3 tablespoons lightly packed fresh mint leaves *or* 1 tablespoon dried mint
3 tablespoons lime juice
16 fluid ounces (450ml) carbonated water
Ice cubes

Remove crown from pineapple. Cut off the peel. Halve pineapple lengthwise; cut out core. Finely chop pineapple (should measure about 1 pint plus 4 fluid ounces (570ml). Place chopped pineapple or *undrained* tinned pineapple in a 2-quart (2 litre) saucepan. Add sugar and 8 fluid ounces (225ml) *water*. Bring to boiling; reduce heat. Cover and simmmer for 15 minutes.

◀ ***Pictured opposite: Seafood Tabbouleh, Minty Pineappleade, and Lemon Bread***

Meanwhile, tie fresh or dried mint in a piece of cheesecloth. Place mint bag in pineapple mixture. Let stand, covered, about 1½ hours or till slightly cool. strain; discard mint. Reserve the pineaple for another use. Stir lime juice into pineapple liquid. Pour into jars or an airtight container. Cover and chill.

Before serving, slowly add carbonated water. Serve over ice cubes. Garnish with pineapple wedges and fresh mint leaves, if desired. Makes about 1 quart (1 litre).

***Note:** If you're using tinned pineapple, reduce the amount of water to 6 fluid ounces (170ml).

Seafood Tabbouleh

5 ounces (140g) bulgur wheat
12 ounces (345g) frozen crab meat and prawns, thawed
1 medium cucumber, seeded and finely chopped
¼ ounce (7g) snipped parsley
1½ ounces (40g) thinly sliced spring onion
2 fluid ounces (55ml) salad oil
2 fluid ounces (55ml) lemon juice
1 tablespoon snipped fresh mint *or* 1 teaspoon dried mint, crushed
¼ teaspoon salt
⅛ teaspoon pepper
1 medium tomato, seeded and chopped
Tomato rose (optional)
Mint leaves (optional)

Place bulgur in a colander. Rinse with cold water. Drain well. In a large bowl combine drained bulgur, crab meat and prawns, cucumber, parsley, and onion. For dressing, in a screw top jar combine oil, lemon juice, snipped mint, salt, and pepper. Cover and shake well. Pour over bulgur mixture. Toss to coat. Cover and chill overnight.

Before serving, stir in chopped tomato. Garnish with a tomato rose and mint leaves, if desired. Makes 6 main-dish servings.

Greens Galore

A salad overflowing with fresh greens is the perfect way to enjoy garden-fresh flavour year-round. Although round and garden lettuces remain popular choices among salad lovers, it's fun to be daring and explore what other greens have to offer. Add pizzazz to your next salad by using a combination of greens that differ in flavour, texture, and colour. We've simplified things for you a bit. Here's information on how to identify and select your greens.

Green beginnings
Choosing greens is the first step in making any salad memorable. Select the freshest greens possible, avoiding limp or bruised greens. Don't wash until needed. Then, when ready to use, wash, drain, and pat greens dry. Place leftovers in a polythene bag or covered container to keep them crisp. Store in the refrigerator.

To serve, tear leaves to expose the insides and allow the greens to absorb the dressing. Cutting them bruises and discolours the leaves.

Cos lettuce
Cos lettuce originated on the Greek island of Cos. This lettuce has elongated, coarse leaves with a heavy rib running down the middle of each leaf. Leaves near the outside of the head are long and large; the centre leaves are more tender and delicate. Cos lettuce is crisp, with a refreshingly pungent flavour.

Leaf lettuce

Webb's Wonder lettuce

Round lettuce

Garden
Garden lettuce is often confused with round lettuce. Garden is a medium, round-headed lettuce with soft, waxy leaves. In keeping with its delicate appearance, garden lettuce has a delicate, mild flavour.

Round
Round lettuce is shaped similar to garden lettuce and is a member of the butterhead family. Round lettuce is somewhat smaller than garden lettuce. The small, cup-shaped leaves have a soft, delicate texture and lend a subtly sweet flavour to salads. These small, tender leaves also make attractive serving containers and plate liners for individual servings of salad.

Webb's Wonder
A most popular salad green is Webb's Wonder, also called crisphead or head lettuce. When shopping for this salad favourite, look for a solid, compact head with tight leaves. The leaves will vary from pale green in the centre to medium green on the outside. Webb's Wonder, one of the crispest lettuces, has a mild, watery flavour, so it nicely complements salads containing stronger greens.

Leaf
There are several types of leaf lettuce. The flavour is similar in all of them, but the leaves may be green to bronze to red-tipped. When selecting any type of leaf lettuce, look for large, leafy bunches of lettuce with tender leaves. The sweet yet delicate flavour blends well in any salad.

Escarole

Endive

More Glorious Greens

If you're unfamiliar with names like escarole, sorrel, or watercress, you're not alone. Because these greens are not as readily available and well-known as others, you might not know how delicious they are. Browse through this section and then sample some of these special greens in your next salad.

Escarole
Coming from the endive family, escarole is often known as broad-leafed endive. Escarole has broader, less curly leaves than endive. Escarole's colour can range from dark green to pale yellow.

When purchasing escarole, choose leaves that are fresh and tender. This coarse-textured green will add a slightly bitter flavour to your salads.

Endive
Endive, sometimes known as Frisée, is a prickly textured green that adds zest to salads, with its somewhat sharp flavour. In addition to adding pep, this green is loaded with vitamin A.

Look for endive with narrow, curly leaves. Endive combines well with milder greens.

Spinach

Sorrel

Watercress

Rocket

Spinach
Spinach has often been reputed to be the vegetable that builds muscles and strength. It's true that this vegetable is full of vitamins and iron—and it's also delicous both cooked and raw.

When used raw, as a salad green, the dark green leaves add colour and character to a salad. Available year-round, spinach should have dark green leaves that are crisp and free of moisture and mould.

Watercress
As the name suggests, watercress grows in freshwater ponds and streams. This pungently flavoured green is a lively addition to any salad. Look for large, dark green leaves. As a rule, the darker and larger the leaves, the better the watercress.

Watercress can also serve as an attractive, edible garnish.

Sorrel
Sorrel, also known as sourgrass, looks almost like spinach, but the leaves are somewhat smaller. Sorrel, however, is not as common as spinach and may require some extra shopping effort.

Look for young, tender sorrel leaves that are free from blemishes. Sorrel's lemony flavour gives a sharp, slightly acidic taste to salads.

Rocket
Rocket, also known as arugula, is Italian in origin. While this green is often hard to find, taking the extra time to search for it is worth it. Its dark green leaves lend a peppery flavour to any salad. Choose young, tender leaves for the best flavour.

Oil Options

No matter what you're preparing—a creamy mayonnaise dressing or a sophisticated vinaigrette—it's always important to select an oil that will enhance each salad individually. By learning to identify different types of oils, you can choose an oil that complements your salad.

Nut-Flavoured Oil

7½ ounces (215g) unblanched shelled whole hazelnuts, almonds, *or* walnuts
1 pint (550ml) salad oil

Place nuts in a blender container or food processor bowl. Cover and blend or process till chopped. Through the opening in the lid, and with the blender on slow speed, gradully add 4 fluid ounces (115ml) of oil. Blend till nuts are finely chopped.

Transfer nut mixture to a saucepan. Place a candy thermometer in the pan. Cook over low heat, stirring occasionally, till thermometer registers 160°F (70°C). Remove from heat; cool slightly. Combine nut mixture with remaining oil. Cover tightly; let stand in a cool place for 1 to 2 weeks.

Line a colander with fine-woven cloth or cup-shaped coffee filter. Pour oil mixture through colander; let drain in a bowl. Discard nut paste. Pour strained oil into a 1 pint (550ml) jar; cover tightly. Refrigerate up to 3 months.

Walnut oil
Peanut oil
Sesame oil

Vegetable Oils
Because of their subtle flavours these all-purpose oils are used in the kitchen for baking and frying. They also work well in salads where other flavours dominate. The most common vegetable oils are corn, safflower, sunflower, rapeseed, coconut, and soybean.

Hazelnut Oil
Hazelnut oil, also called filbert oil, is a golden-coloured oil. Like walnut oil, it has a unique, nutty flavour.

Olive Oil
The colour of olive oil ranges from golden to a greenish hue. Spanish and Greek olive oils tend to be stronger than Italian or French oils. Olive oil flavours range from fruity and mellow to sharply distinct.

The finest olive oil is labelled "extra virgin". This oil has less than one percent of oleic acid. "Virgin" has slightly lower standards with a higher oleic acid content. Because these oils have not been heat-treated or preserved, they should be kept for only a month or two.

Almond Oil
Almond oil is a clear, pale oil. Its delicate flavour adds interest to salad dressings.

Walnut Oil
This is a rich, golden-coloured oil. It contributes a nutty flavour to some dressings, but is too harsh for strong-flavoured dressings. It is not recommended for frying or baking.

Peanut Oil
Peanut oil is also referred to as groundnut oil. It blends well in salad dressings because of its delicate flavour. or, use it for frying—it's odourless.

Sesame Oil
There are two types of sesame oil. One, a thick, brown oil, is made from toasted sesame seed. It has a concentrated flavour and is used in very small amounts to flavour dressings.

The other type of sesame seed oil is pale yellow and is made from untoasted sesame seed. Its bland flavour is good for salads with stronger flavours.

Mint vinegar

Tarragon vinegar

Garlic vinegar

Flavoured Vinegars

Flavoured vinegars are making a comeback. Why? Because they add character to salads, sauces, marinades, soups, and stews. These vinegars are a delicious way to add pizzazz to your favourite dishes. Look for your favourite flavoured vinegar in the store, or try making your own.

Raspberry Vinegar

- **10 ounces (285g) fresh raspberries *or* frozen raspberries, thawed and drained**
- **1½ pints (825ml) white wine or cider vinegar**
- **16 fluid ounces (450ml) dry red wine**

Rinse fresh raspberries with cold water and drain well. In a large bowl combine raspberries, white wine vinegar, and wine. Cover and let stand overnight. In a stainless steel or enamel saucepan heat vinegar mixture to boiling; boil, uncovered, for 3 minutes. Cool.

Strain mixture, discarding solids. Pour into bottles; cover tightly. Let the vinegar age for 2 to 4 weeks before using. Store in cool, dark place. Makes about 2½ pints (1 litre, 420ml).

Vinegar beginnings
Distilled, cider, and wine vinegar are the three most common vinegars for making flavoured vinegars. Distilled vinegar is a colourless vinegar made from grain mash. The distilling process removes any flavour and leaves only an acidic taste. Cider vinegar, made from apples, is a golden-brown vinegar with a slightly fruity flavour. In wine vinegars the colour and flavour of the vinegar depends on the type of wine used. White wine produces a lighter-tasting vinegar than red wine.

Vinegar variety
To make flavoured vinegars, start with a base of cider, distilled, or wine vinegar. Your choice of a base depends on how you plan to flavour your vinegar. Wine vinegars are good with herbs and spices. Fruits and edible flowers go well with distilled and white wine vinegars. Try using cider vinegar with spices.

How to flavour vinegars
Flavoured vinegars can be prepared in two ways. The quickest method is heating the vinegar in a stainless steel or enamel pan until hot, but not boiling. Pour the vinegar over the herbs, seed, fruit, or spice. Cover with cheesecloth and let stand in a warm, dark place for one to two weeks. Then, filter the vinegar through several layers of cheesecloth and pour it into bottles. Or, pour the vinegar directly over the ingredients and let it stand for a month.

When sampling vinegar, trust your taste buds. If the vinegar is too strong, add some plain vinegar. If it's too weak, add some seasoning. Once you've tried a variety of vinegars, try combining flavours. Mix two or three ingredients, like raspberry and mint, lemon and garlic, or peaches and cloves.

Nutrition Analysis Chart

Use these analyses to compare nutritional values of different recipes. This information was calculated using Agriculture Handbook Number 456, published by the United States Department of Agriculture, as the primary source.

In compiling the nutriton analyses, we made the following assumptions:

- For all of the main-dish meat recipes, the nutrition analyses were calculated using weights and measures for cooked meat.
- Garnishes and optional ingredients were not included in the nutrition analyses.
- If a marinade was brushed over a food during cooking, the analysis includes all of the marinade.
- When two ingredient options appear in a recipe, calculations were made using the first one.
- For ingredients of variable weight (such as "2½- to 3-pound (1 to 1½kg) broiler-fryer chicken") or for recipes with a serving range ("Makes 4 to 6 servings"), calculations were made using the first figure.

	Per Serving						U.S. Recommended Daily Allowances Per Serving (%)							
	Calories	Protein (g)	Carbohydrate (g)	Fat (g)	Sodium (mg)	Potassium (mg)	Protein	Vitamin A	Vitamin C	Thiamine	Riboflavin	Niacin	Calcium	Iron
Main-Dish Salads														
Avocado and Egg Salad (p.29)	501	17	8	46	555	689	25	31	26	14	27	8	8	18
Beef 'n' Swiss Salad (p.99)	399	18	4	35	352	335	27	66	35	5	17	8	33	14
B.L.T. Salad (p.99)	426	21	12	33	413	576	33	34	41	14	16	25	7	18
Broccoli-Salmon Salad (p.26)	384	27	6	28	229	756	41	29	67	6	18	44	25	10
Cheesy Prawn Salad (p.28)	427	25	7	34	462	374	39	25	47	6	22	5	54	12
Chicken and Curry Salad (p.47)	544	25	22	41	364	669	38	19	17	9	12	40	7	16
Chicken Salad in Tortilla Bowls (p.92)	389	27	25	21	215	599	42	30	78	9	24	41	12	18
Confetti Tuna Salad (p.28)	193	18	7	10	540	481	28	65	12	9	9	35	6	10
Creamy Chicken-and-Rice Salad (p.69)	333	21	27	15	503	531	32	24	28	17	14	31	10	14
Crunchy Chicken Salad (p.98)	486	30	11	37	447	743	47	72	182	13	17	41	10	19
Curried Prawn Salad (p.105)	339	20	29	15	398	408	31	14	33	14	10	19	13	14
Fruited Chicken Salad (p.29)	517	26	32	34	311	834	40	20	28	13	16	37	5	16
Ham and Broad Bean Salad (p.68)	613	20	41	41	954	421	30	17	57	29	14	19	6	21
Ham-Pineapple Salad (p.28)	260	16	13	16	542	358	25	4	31	28	13	14	6	12
Ham Slaw Salad (p.111)	235	11	6	19	445	281	17	25	69	18	8	10	4	9
Herbed Ham and Asparagus Salad (p.104)	243	34	10	13	454	631	35	29	41	24	24	30	8	19
Layered Reuben Salad (p.44)	617	26	19	50	1147	342	40	23	41	9	24	11	33	22
Mix and Match Chef's Salad (p.98)	414	20	8	34	642	559	31	49	27	21	23	15	32	15
Pepperoni Salad (p.105)	236	10	16	15	622	430	15	50	21	12	10	9	8	13
Robust Beef Salad (p.104)	246	20	11	14	478	436	30	33	32	7	19	10	35	17
Salmon Salad in Bread Bowls (p.93)	566	37	57	22	1170	835	57	14	15	25	23	62	35	30
Scallop Salad with Pineapple Dressing (p.103)	228	23	26	5	393	493	36	17	33	12	10	7	14	20
Seafood Salad (p.97)	423	23	13	32	341	920	36	41	53	13	19	22	13	21

	Per Serving						U.S. Recommended Daily Allowances Per Serving (%)							
	Calories	Protein (g)	Carbohydrate (g)	Fat (g)	Sodium (mg)	Potassium (mg)	Protein	Vitamin A	Vitamin C	Thiamine	Riboflavin	Niacin	Calcium	Iron
Main-Dish Salads *(continued)*														
Scampi and Spaetzle Salad (p.63)	319	20	23	17	365	380	31	57	48	12	12	13	13	22
Seafood Tabbouleh (p.113)	223	12	24	10	93	203	6	13	35	7	4	8	3	9
Tarragon-Chicken Salad (p.104)	275	27	13	13	443	538	41	67	25	11	19	28	29	15
Side-Dish Salads														
All-American Layered Salad (p.42)	556	11	11	53	609	355	17	88	28	15	14	7	22	13
Apple-Orange Salad (p.47)	204	5	20	13	64	396	8	33	43	18	9	5	7	11
Apple-Raisin Salad (p.80)	150	3	37	0	72	240	4	3	5	2	2	1	2	6
Asparagus and Pasta Salad (p.60)	199	6	22	10	174	326	10	21	46	9	7	7	7	9
Avocado Fruit Freeze (p.32)	248	3	30	14	45	332	4	11	18	6	9	4	4	3
Beetroot-Spinach Salad (p.10)	179	5	11	14	647	509	8	136	75	6	13	3	11	17
Berry-Stuffed Papayas (p.90)	188	3	35	6	14	601	4	55	171	11	8	5	7	7
Blue Cheese Garden Salad (p.55)	259	7	12	22	337	530	11	182	184	11	21	7	17	10
Broccoli-Mushroom Salad (p.17)	96	3	7	7	102	315	5	23	93	6	14	8	5	6
Burgundy-Grape Mould (p.80)	266	4	44	8	59	151	6	8	79	5	6	2	4	5
Caesar Salad (p.108)	109	4	6	8	98	153	6	21	18	4	6	2	9	6
Caraway Cabbage Salad (p.38)	106	1	6	9	104	195	2	8	76	3	2	1	3	3
Cavatelli-Artichoke Salad (p.61)	532	16	80	18	219	569	25	19	35	63	37	37	8	22
Chutney Salad (p.10)	119	4	17	5	34	325	6	21	17	5	6	9	7	8
Confetti Salad in Pepper Shells (p.92)	127	9	8	7	214	293	14	31	179	6	13	3	7	5
Cranberry-Nog Mould (p.83)	242	5	46	5	72	152	7	5	12	2	8	1	9	2
Cranberry-Orange Salad (p.74)	189	2	45	1	46	69	3	1	30	1	1	0	1	2
Cranberry-Pear Salad (p.22)	123	1	31	1	3	202	2	2	35	4	3	1	2	3
Creamy Macaroni-Fruit Salad (p.61)	192	3	24	10	18	185	5	9	14	10	6	3	3	5
Creamy Potato Salad (p.52)	367	5	24	29	706	532	7	6	32	8	6	8	3	7
Crouton Salad Bowl (p.10)	181	6	8	15	302	259	9	20	12	4	7	2	17	11
Crunchy Coleslaw with Creamy Dressing (p.16)	88	1	5	7	155	172	2	24	71	3	4	2	4	3
Crunchy Coleslaw with Vinaigrette Dressing (p.16)	63	1	5	5	58	170	2	23	71	3	4	2	3	2
Curried Fruit Salad (p.44)	292	5	63	5	58	744	7	17	39	14	13	6	10	11
Date Waldorf Salad (p.22)	279	3	29	19	99	344	4	6	36	7	4	3	5	7
Dilled Vegetable Combo (p.39)	115	2	7	10	108	223	3	63	43	5	4	3	3	5
Dilled Vegetable Vinaigrette (p.52)	112	3	11	7	41	571	4	94	35	8	17	15	3	8
Easy Apricot Salad (p.23)	186	3	28	8	28	384	5	26	25	8	9	4	7	6
Fiesta Salad (p.45)	213	9	15	14	478	231	13	9	11	3	7	3	17	7
French-Onion Fling (p.10)	230	3	13	19	393	244	4	4	6	3	7	5	1	3
Fresh Fruit Platter (p.111)	230	1	17	18	1	176	1	5	64	5	3	2	2	4
Frosty Tropical Salads (p.33)	223	4	14	18	79	230	6	16	11	5	7	2	4	4
Fruit and Rice Salad (p.69)	208	4	26	10	163	200	7	7	8	9	4	11	4	6
Fruit-filled Nectarines (p.92)	143	1	38	0	19	511	2	51	46	3	6	8	2	6
Fruity Pasta Salad (p.63)	125	4	26	1	25	212	5	13	34	11	7	7	2	6
Ginger Fruit Bowl (p.20)	190	3	32	7	55	545	4	15	219	8	12	8	9	14
Golden Salad (p.75)	189	3	47	0	72	248	4	4	17	5	2	1	2	4
Grape and Pineapple Salad (p.47)	97	2	15	4	14	189	2	6	11	4	4	2	4	3
Greek Layered Salad (p.45)	87	5	6	5	317	257	8	43	30	5	8	3	14	9
Greek-Style Salad (p.11)	108	3	7	9	168	166	4	46	27	3	4	1	7	7

	Per Serving						U.S. Recommended Daily Allowances Per Serving (%)							
	Calories	Protein (g)	Carbohydrate (g)	Fat (g)	Sodium (mg)	Potassium (mg)	Protein	Vitamin A	Vitamin C	Thiamine	Riboflavin	Niacin	Calcium	Iron
Side-Dish Salads *(continued)*														
Italian Bean and Potato Salad (p.50)	259	6	26	15	488	658	10	10	39	13	13	15	7	8
Layered Vegetable Aspic (p.78)	80	7	11	2	521	134	10	24	29	6	3	10	2	4
Lime and Grape Salad (p.74)	107	2	26	0	47	177	3	1	4	2	1	1	1	2
Marinated Mushrooms (p.38)	94	2	6	7	193	354	4	4	39	6	17	14	2	5
Mushroom-and-Bacon Rice Salad (p.68)	148	3	14	9	167	189	5	5	15	8	9	9	1	5
Mushroom-Avocado Stuffed Tomatoes (p.93)	260	3	11	24	180	775	5	27	64	11	15	13	3	7
Oriental Rice Salad (p.66)	158	4	20	8	198	75	6	3	8	7	7	6	2	7
Oriental Toss (p.11)	98	1	7	8	155	131	2	11	13	2	3	1	2	5
Parsnip Salad (p.17)	141	2	14	9	338	403	3	3	61	4	5	1	5	4
Perky Potato Salad (p.53)	189	2	16	14	138	394	3	8	49	6	3	7	2	4
Plum-Banana Salad (p.23)	168	1	39	3	6	388	2	15	27	3	4	5	2	4
Potato and Beetroot Salad (p.55)	202	3	26	11	276	517	4	4	35	7	4	7	3	7
Rum Fruit Moulds (p.81)	133	2	21	4	47	155	3	9	2	3	1	2	1	3
Shells and Cheeses Salad (p.60)	400	16	26	26	398	247	25	17	19	19	21	10	29	9
Snappy Tomato Cubes (p.75)	136	4	25	3	242	305	6	16	39	4	4	4	4	5
Spiced Fruit Salad (p.39)	111	1	28	1	3	313	2	15	90	4	6	5	2	6
Strawberry and Apple Salad (p.72)	141	2	35	0	70	176	3	1	5	1	1	0	1	4
Summertime Melon-Lime Mould (p.83)	146	2	36	0	9	161	3	1	24	2	1	2	1	2
Sweet 'n' Sour Salad (p.16)	109	2	14	6	13	208	3	44	19	8	3	3	3	6
Sweet Potato and Pecan Salad (p.52)	321	5	35	19	352	490	8	194	59	17	9	5	8	8
Tater Salad (p.53)	180	4	36	3	539	368	7	20	76	7	6	6	3	7
Three-Bean Carrot Salad (p.36)	255	4	21	19	279	349	6	125	68	6	6	4	7	14
Three-Fruit Salad (p.22)	127	1	33	0	3	280	2	19	79	3	5	5	2	6
Tomato-Parmesan Toss (p.8)	139	4	7	11	360	234	5	20	23	5	6	3	8	6
Tortellini and Cucumber Salad (p.58)	323	10	24	21	456	251	15	8	16	22	10	10	17	11
Vegetable Potpourri (p.14)	127	3	9	10	129	339	4	27	76	5	6	4	6	4
Very Berry Puff (p.74)	91	3	20	0	67	103	5	0	0	1	4	0	6	0
Wilted Chinese Cabbage Salad (p.87)	138	5	12	8	549	511	7	59	79	12	10	7	7	13
Wilted Cos Salad (p.86)	107	2	8	8	83	236	3	24	54	7	4	3	5	6
Zippy Gazpacho Moulds (p.81)	26	3	4	0	185	246	4	13	30	4	2	4	2	3
Miscellaneous														
Cooked Salad Dressing (p.102)	25	1	3	1	78	19	1	2	0	1	2	0	2	1
Creamy Mayonnaise (p.96)	101	0	0	11	56	5	1	1	1	0	0	0	0	0
Herb Twists (p.111)	198	5	30	6	569	74	8	2	0	12	11	8	6	8
Lemon Bread (p.113)	129	2	21	4	113	36	3	1	1	6	5	4	4	3
Minty Pineappleade (p.113)	164	0	43	0	1	103	0	1	22	4	1	1	1	2
Nut-Flavoured Oil (p.118)	142	1	1	15	0	46	2	0	0	1	3	1	1	2
Raspberry Vinegar (p.120)	7	0	1	0	0	19	0	0	1	0	0	0	0	1

G-L

M-O

P-Q